Royal Feast

A Literary Recipe

Poetry
Prose
Short Stories

Compliments
of
Food4Thot

OSHEA KWA LUJA

Royal Feast

Still Waters Publishing
Royal Feast: A Literary Recipe
All Rights Reserved.
Copyright © 2015
Oshea Kwa Luja (Food4Thot)

This book may not be reproduced, transmitted, or stored, in whole or in part, by any means, including graphics, electronic or mechanical, without the expressed written consent of the author/publisher, except in the case of brief quotations embodied in critical articles and reviews.

Published by Still Waters Publishing
First Printed 2015
ISBN - 13: 978-0692393406
ISBN - 10: 0692393404
Printed in the United States of America

Royal Feast

Royal Feast

A Literary Recipe

Poetry
Prose
Short Stories

Compliments
of
Food4 Thot

OSHEA KWA LUJA

Royal Feast

"No individual has any right to come into the world and go out of it without leaving behind him distinct and legitimate reasons for having passed through it."

-George Washington Carver

Royal Feast

The Invitation

Food4Thot should be your first resort if it's knowledge that you seek. So pick up his book and take a look, then listen to it speak.

A gourmet for every day, until your mind is well fed, as you sift through its pages and read sagas of Black sages to the living, by the dead—who were all ancestors of today's descendants of slaves who still speak to and through their progeny, from beyond their graves.

This isn't mere chatter, but mind over matter, from a buffet to a snack; listening A to Z by Chef Triple B, and each B stands for Black.

Illuminating, invigorating, and placating your appetites, about what's going down, from city to town, and the wrongs disguised as rights. And as you read on, the words will become strong, and imbedded in your mind, until you know all about yourself, stolen wealth, and natural health, from a recipe that came forward from behind, in space and time.

A five-course meal that will appeal to your taste for freedom's thought, until you start synching and readjusting your thinking into realizing ... whatever you've missed, he's caught.

You don't even need a venue; just scan the menu to take out whichever dish you wish; and then satisfy your will to eat your fill, and drink whatever you think about Black acts that are factual and episodes that were actual, as your eyes check the list.

Royal Feast

Soon, your mental health will return after you've learned the truth about self and kind, which had lain submerged until it re-emerged from the recesses of the mind.

It's Black vintage lineage, like collard greens instead of spinach, that will cause you to belch, burp, or fart; and you'll not only see eye to eye, but also know how and why, self-love is still in your heart.

Five stars is my review. For you to know what you once knew, just take in all you see by Chef Triple B, because I and you are part of his crew, and Food4Thot is He.

Oh, and by the way, don't forget to tip the waiter, sooner rather than later—that is, if you cater to this restaurant. In fact, it's so Black, it may become your favorite haunt!

- **Jalal Nuriddin**
of The Last Poets

The Kitchen

For me, what makes a great kitchen is the love you prepare your food with, and the tantalizing flavors and aromas you are able to extract from the process of cooking. The taste of food changes according to the herbs and seasoning you include. Cayenne pepper adds heat, chamomile softens the blow, rosemary and thyme enhance the flavor, and all of them are healing in their own special way.

I would like to thank all of the seasonings that added spices and flavors to this Royal Feast. To the matriarch and patriarch of my family, Ruby and Franklin Alexander, thank you for being the rosemary that has strengthened my memory, my safe place to gather childhood memories from and write. To my dandelion and licorice root, Barbara Montgomery and Otis Perry, my parents, who showed me how to live life courageous and strong, without seeking approval. A royal embrace to my children, my five dimensions of essential seasoning, you all are life's most precious treasures, and at times, I sit puzzled, feeling inadequate for being blessed with such beloved beings.

A benevolent bow of gratefulness to my wife Melanie, my wildflower and saffron, who has rejuvenated and restored my purpose and passion for creating. So blessed I am to be sharing this journey with you! Many thanks and praises to Father Amde Hamilton, my sage, the promoter of growth and wisdom, thank you for our endless conversations on family, poetry, and Watts. It's been truly an honor to sit with, listen to, and learn from one of the greats!

Royal Feast

And to my sweet basil, S. Pearl Sharp, the one who always said, "Are you sure you want to say it that way?" Thank you for all you've done for my artistry.

A big salute to Baba Jalal, my medicinal herb, who has helped to alleviate artistic congestion with a cosmic twist. And thank you to my manuscript's editor, Charlene E. Green, who's the cloves behind this project. She helped to increase circulation when the flow would slow down. Thank you for your patience and professionalism.

To my hometown, the city of Watts, my soil, my fertile grounds, my inspiration for becoming a poet ... thank you for the many spices, herbs, and flavors you've added to my experiences that are reflected through my work. I am proud to be one of your offspring!

And last but not least, my kelp, mustard seed, bee-pollen stimulant, the poetry community ... all of the poets, artists, venues, and wonderful people I've met along this journey, naming all of you would go on forever, so I'll give an enormous, broad-sweeping energy of thanks and reverence for all of you!

-Food4Thot

Libation

Libation is a revered Afrakan ritual practiced throughout the world. It is a drink offering to every category of beings and elements in the cosmos, yet every group may not be addressed in all libation accounts. A libation generally pays homage to the Most High, along with calling forth the names of lesser divinities, honorable ancestors, and our beloved habitat, which is Mother Earth.

The libation is the most important part of any feast or ceremony, and must be presented with the utmost reverence for its energy alone. After each ancestor's name is called, water or liquid is poured onto the ground, stage, or plant to represent Mother Earth, and the attendees respond with asè (ah-shay), which means "so it is," similar to amen. The subsequent libation is meant to usher us into this Royal Feast.

(Dear Mother/Father Spirit, the Most High, incorruptible divine being that reflects His/Her light in all that is, we pour libation in honor of your energy, spirit, and covering, asè! We pour libation for Mother Earth, our first form of vegetation and harvest; we say asè. We pour libation for the first hands to ever prepare a meal in Afraka; we say asè. We pour libation for the ancestors that were already here in the Americas, cooking and feeding their village before the invasion; we say asè! We pour libation for our ancestors that were kidnapped and brought over to the Americas in chains and to be sold as slaves, and for those ancestors who dove into the Atlantic and drowned rather than to witness the horrific acts against us as a people; we say asè! We pour libation for the numerous enslaved black cooks that fed the early so-called founding fathers of America: James Hemings, Dolly Johnson, Mary Campbell, Vietta Garr, and Zephyr Wright; we say asè. We pour libation for George Washington Carver, the first to discover the many uses of the peanut, sweet potatoes, and the soy bean; we say asè. We pour libation for the first black cooks and farmers who got us through slavery and Jim Crow; we say asè.

We pour libation for the injustice overthrowers, those men and women who led anti-slavery revolutions: Nat Turner, Harriet Tubman, Toussaint L'Ouverture, Sojourner Truth; we say asè! We pour libation for the great freedom fighters and Black Nationalists: Marcus Garvey, Malcolm X, Dr. Martin Luther King Jr.; we say asè!

We pour libation for the poets and writers that have scribed our existence on many scrolls: Phillis Wheatley, Arna Bontemps, Jayne Cortez, Wanda Coleman, Richard Dedeaux; we say asè!

We pour libation for our family, grandmothers, grandfathers, Mrs. Addie Mae Moffett, Willie Moffett, Barbara West; we say asè! We pour libation for your personal ancestors that have covered you, the reader, from all evil, harm, and danger. List names below...

_____
_____
_____

We say asè! Asè! Asè!)

Royal Feast

The Menu

Royal Feast

Eat responsibly...

Royal Feast

The Recipe - by Food4Thot

Appetizers

-Birth, Education, Sankofa-

Arrival / 15
Offspring's Vantage / 16
You From / 17
Shallow Education / 19
In Formation / 21
Sequoia / 23
If the Shoe Fits / 24
Poetry / 25
Forward Ever / 26
Natural Pearl / 27
Stage Left / 29

Super Food

-Life, Love, Legacy-

5th Dimension / 33
Give Thanks / 35
333 Seconds / 37
Her, Me, We / 39
We Be Chosen / 41
Barbara / 44
Father Like Sun / 45
Cosmic Balance / 46
Purple Analysis / 47
Black Spirit / 48

Royal Feast

November Whispers / 49
Rain Woman / 50
Pops / 51
Community / 53

Entrees

-Loyalty, Truth, Our-Story-

Royal Feast / 57
The Darker Brother / 63
Old School / 67
Me Be Poet / 71
Ancient / 73
Who I Be / 77
Eclectic Expressions / 83
Flowers / 85
Turn the Page / 87

Wine & Spirits

- Watts, CA -

Ease In / 91
Wizard of Watts (Baba Amde) / 93
Mother Watts #2 / 95
I Know These Parts #1 / 96
I Know These Parts #2 / 97
I Know These Parts #3 / 99
Big City, Bright Lights / 101
We Be Watts Fathers / 103
Ride / 105
Tribal Chant / 107

Royal Feast

Hard Liquor

- Straight Shots, No Chaser -

Shots Fired / 111
Forgiveness / 112
Flagrant & Foul / 113
Don't Call / 114
A Problem / 115
The Scene / 116
Young Hopeful / 117
Foggy Mirrors / 120
Pardon My Tears / 121
Whom It May Concern / 123

Desserts

-Bitter, Sweet, Tasty, Complete-

The Fireplace / 127
Destiny's Certainty / 129
Prepare for Takeoff! / 130
Wake Up / 131
Independence / 133
Thinking / 134
Soul Mate / 135
Questions / 136
Myths / 137
Rain Forest / 138
Dark Matter / 139

Royal Feast

*Youthful Steps / **140***
*M.J. / **141***
*Whole / **142***
*Mind's Eye / **143***
*No Defeat / **144***
*An Olmec's Sankofa / **145***
*Casualties / **146***

<u>*Asè*</u>
-Tributes, Honors, Reflections-

*For Richard Dedeaux / **149***
*Dee Black / **151***
*For Jessica Cleaves / **153***
*Tribute to a King / **155***
*Baba Baraka / **157***
*Breast Cancer (Breast Can Serve) / **159***
*For Bee / **161***
*Latasha Harlins / **163***
*Borrowed Angel (Devin) / **165***
*That Dude (Stephan A. Grays) / **167***

<u>*Champagne*</u>
-A Toast to Spoken Word-
(My Poetry Thread) / 171

*Lookin' for Me / **183***

About the Chef / 185

Royal Feast

Dedicated to **Love**...

I
could not
have done this
without you!

Royal Feast

"When you are hungry, the description of food does not feed you. But most of us are satisfied with the description of truth."

-Jiddu Krishnamurti

The Recipe

Biltmore brim tilted over right lazy eye; legs crossed V-style as aged hands grip an antique porcelain coffee mug housing Folgers dark roast. It's 5:30a.m. The city's resting and Grandpa is enjoying a still morning while browsing through the *Herald Examiner* newspaper. "Lakers Win the Championship!"

The year is 1980. A new decade of victories and losses would define this era of crack cocaine, big hair, and pop music. In less than four years, I'd discover my love for poetry, and my beloved grandpa would become an untimely ancestor.

Mr. Clean, as the neighborhood of Watts affectionately called him, was known for his spotless threads, dashikis, and Stacy Adams shoes. He and his wife, Addie Mae Moffett (my grandmother), owned two soul-food restaurants, The Green Room Café and The Blue Diamond; a few bookie joints, a home, and an arsenal of artillery that he reminded the world he had at 12a.m. every New Year's Day. I still remember our last conversation, as I stood outside of his brand-new mint green Ford LTD, while he sat confined to minimum movement on the passenger side, occasionally looking up to see if I was paying attention.

He asked, "Have you ever been to Las Vegas?" I replied, "No, sir."

He told me he was going to take me to Las Vegas and show me around. He also mentioned that the food there was plentiful and delicious. As he spoke, I pictured us there, eating till our stomachs swelled three times the size, all while winning a trillion dollars on the black jack table. He coughed painfully and brought me out of my fantasy trip to Vegas. Something was weakening his strong, manly presence. He began to jump from topic to topic, as if he was giving me a crash course on life before he made his ultimate departure. He warned me against jealous people, saying that I have the gift of light, and many might be intimidated by that expression. "sun," as he would say, "you are a very special boy, and you will go on to do great things, travel the world, and make your family proud. Just never forget where you come from!" Interestingly enough, I began to realize that this might be our last conversation, so I got right to the meat and potatoes.

"Granddad, what makes a good life?" He replied, "Family, good health, and great food!"

"Family, good health, and great food," I repeated, thinking, *wow*, at age eight I was living the good life. My family was together, our health was pretty good, and great food was a ritual we came to expect in our family.

Essentially, great food was the springboard for breaking bread, bonding while eating together, and sharing a practice that dates back thousands of years, which represented a majestic exchange of energy, sovereignty in its purest form. This acknowledgment led me to over-stand that royalty is a spirit, a state of mind that colors radiant hues of splendid into the family's fabric. When complemented with Watts's historical temperature and sprinkled with my family's abundant sharing of provisions, it had lent itself to this manuscript's title, *Royal Feast*.

Nearly every family that moved to Watts from the South in those times brought with them a tradition of down South soul-food cooking. Food was our medication, the thread that weaved generations together, sparking great jokes and teachable moments. Children sat and listened, only chiming in if they were asked a question.

Watts, a.k.a Mud Town, is the city my family settled in once they arrived from Florida, Arkansas, and Texas during the second great migration, in search of better opportunities on the West Coast. World War II had the weapons and industrial industries booming, and Watts had several manufacturing plants in walking distance of the residents. So it became an open secret that if you were looking for employment, great weather year-round, and homeownership, then Watts, CA, was the place to be.

Watts had a thriving underground community as well, made up of many lively characters that, at any given moment, would go to an extreme. I watched my grandpa handle all of these characters with a stern, loving touch. Since he was also a chef, he would bless everyone with great food and good conversation. My grandpa had a way of simplifying the complex, bringing order to chaos. He was "cooler than the other side of the mattress," the very reason my family came to Watts in the first place. He would always find opportunity in the most obscure situations, and reason from the things others found difficulty in. He was a very resourceful man that would go to the ends of earth to provide for his family.

Cooking was celebrated in my family, stagnation was frowned upon, and we were taught at an early age to adapt, adjust, and thrive in whatever situation we were confronted with. My grandpa also told me that a man does not wait for change; he goes out and creates it.

As a child growing up in Watts, I remember feeling anxious for Sunday dinner. My whole family would come together at the dining room table to eat, laugh, and interlace dysfunction into a quilt of harmony, an understanding of why and how we became what we were as a family.

Old sayings were also passed from one generation to the next, as we, the children, would look baffled at what was just said, like, "You can take a mule to the water, but you can't make him drink," and "I brought you into this world and I will take you out!" or, one of my favorites, "I brought the pumpkin to town; you're the one trying to sell it." What? Okay, it took me awhile to over-stand that one. I later realized that these nuggets of wisdom would become my first introduction to "food for thought."

I began to develop an appetite for witty sayings from the old-timers that had been through a life of struggle and whose faces showed intense living. I would listen closely, absorbing the utterings of these pool-hall sages, backyard shamans, Watts, CA kings and queens who took time to offer me a good word, an embrace, and heartfelt stories of inspiration that adolescent ears were still able to decode and find the lesson in. Similar to the saying, "You can't get butter from a duck," meaning, no matter how much you press for butter from ducks, it will be to no avail, because butter comes from milk and not from ducks, this verbiage began to shape my love for a homegrown dialect that represented an era of straight-up juke-joint talk, no chaser.

I'm from the tutelage of grumpy voices, raspy quotes, and elders coughing to clear their throats before dropping a jewel the size of Mt. Everest on you, while they chewed dinner, drank whisky, and balanced a cigarette hanging off their bottom lip like they forgot it was there. Slacks pressed to the T, and always jingling a pocket full of change, passing out silver to youngins, which was supposed to represent "good fortune." I came up around women who will cuss you out for walking in front of the T.V. "Is yo' daddy a glass maker?" they would ask, with eye glasses resting on the bridge of their noses, snuff close by, a roll of hundred-dollar bills and important documents in their bosom. I used to think the world was in their bosom.

Elderly men kept dice close by, ready to gamble three sixty-five, twenty-four seven. Yet, when the men and women saw me, they always took time to pause and pass a good word, some "food for thought" from the buffets of their minds.

"Listen up, youngsta," as they would say, "nobody is going to give you nothin'! If you want something out of life, go get it!" *GO GET IT* rang in my head for the next few years like an alarm clock attached to my brain. By age seven, I was going to get it, whatever it was. I started running numbers across the street to the bookie joints, memorizing the names of the horses that won, thinking I would bet on the winner when they raced again. To my surprise, they would lose, and the "sure thing" became an anomaly that wasn't sure at all.

The Hollywood racetrack became my fun place as a child. Numbers, money, conversation, and writing became the norm for me. Monday through Saturday was a whirlwind of bustle on my block. However, when Sunday came, everything would cease as our family got prepared for the Karamu, aka the Royal Feast.

Music played a major part in this vibrant, sizzling atmosphere on Sundays after church. We would gather, bless the food, and partake in an array of soul-food entrees. Afterwards, we listened to a record player that belted out Marvin Gaye, Aretha Franklin, and B.B. King's blues and soul tunes as if they were all performing in our living room just for us.

With all of the fun and love my upbringing had to offer, there were also some very difficult times as well. In these hard times, my appetite for expression began to take shape.

I grew up witnessing my mother have three nervous breakdowns before my ninth birthday, our stepfather holding us hostage at gunpoint because it was Thursday, being dropped off to live with an elderly couple we did not know, running away and following the train tracks back to Watts, only to get beat and sent back to this couple's house. Being molested by a woman that was supposed to be babysitting me warped my already distorted perception of relationships at an early age. As a result, I began to stutter tremendously when trying to express myself. It was as though all that I had seen and been through wanted to blurt out of my mouth at once, and my tongue would get tied when trying to express it. What was most interesting was that when I recited poetry or verses from a rap song, I did not stutter.

This is where my fuel for poetry began. By the fourth grade I was in love with writing and being able to shape my vantage from putting pencil to paper. By the fifth grade, I was entrusted with writing the introduction to an animation cartoon our class had created, called *The Project Kids*. The teacher, Ms. Akida Lewis, at Grape St. Elementary School, in Watts, CA, instilled commitment, excellence, and honesty in our work. I credit her for being one of the instruments in my early development as a student and artist. This infinite expression of inscription I was exploring began to guide me towards a few names I would never forget: the Watts Riots, the Watts Writers' Workshop, and the Watts Prophets, in that order.

I first caught wind of the Watts Riots at Mitchell's Barbershop on 112th and Wilmington Avenue, in Watts. I was about ten years of age, tall enough to not need the booster seat in the barber chair. I was receiving my monthly shag haircut when I asked Mitch about the Watts Riots. First, Mr. Mitch explained it was not a riot! He said, "I was there!" It was a rebellion from years of discrimination and brutality from law enforcement and the city of Los Angeles. From that day on, Mr. Mitch showed appreciation for my interest in the history of Watts and would share small nuggets of what he could remember about the historic city.

Like many old-timers at the time, Mr. Mitch kept loads of magazines and newspapers nestled around the 1950s-era designed barbershop for his clients' viewing pleasure. In those days young people would read the paper while waiting to get a haircut, so it was inevitable that one day I would come upon the Watts Writers' Workshop, inside the *Herald Examiner* newspaper, which led me to the West Coast pioneers of rap, The Watts Prophets, and their 1971 album release, *Rappin' Black in a White World*. These occurrences showed me, a young boy growing up in Watts, that I, too, could candidly convey my regards for my community's climate in an artistic way. And since I loved writing, I felt it was my charge to learn all I could about the poets and writers who came before me and were also once children of Watts. What I discovered was absolutely mind-blowing: Watts had a very well-documented history of artists, poets, and musicians whose works had reached monumental proportions in American society.

Transition

One day, while ear hustling on an elder's conversation, I overheard that my grandfather, Mr. Clean, was about to die.

I was shocked, hurt, and disgruntled by the news. So, I chimed in, "What? Die? I thought people lived forever!" My Uncle Toot chuckled and told me, yes, "People do live forever, just not in the physical form." I was confused. Then, he said, "Remember the lessons and stories your grandfather shared with you, and tell others, and that's how he will live forever." At that moment, it clicked. A-ha! I got it!

My grandfather passed in 1983. Shortly thereafter, elders on my block began to transition left and right. A path of legacy had vanished by 1990. One of the last heartbreaks was my grandmother, who passed in 1993, and then my great-grandmother, in 1994. The community was left to us Watts youngstas, a generation of misfits who could not seem to remember any of the lessons, stories, and wisdom that were passed down from our ancestors.

Next, Mr. Mitch got robbed and killed in back of his barbershop. This retired the hope of other youngstas acquiring life lessons from this gem of a man and barbershop. My friends also began to get murdered in and around the Watts area. It was literally a warzone, a concrete bloodbath without any peace convoys to help us deal with this level of calamity. The resources for our community were being misused and directed outside of the community, and as the body count piled up, we were left to figure out what we could not put into words.

Nearly every funeral I attended was of a good friend, so in order to deal with the hurt, I would write a poem about it and share it at my friends' homegoing services. The response was greater than anything I could've ever imagined; families began to request poems from me for their loved ones' funerals. This is where my poetry began to spiral into spoken word, and where I would soon find out that I was entrusted with a gift, a present from the Most High that I had to embrace, explore, and share with all who would listen.

Food4Thot

Writing has been my destiny since birth. I have been through a lengthy initiation process with this ancient inheritance that I do not take lightly. Witnessing my grandmother, Mrs. Addie Mae Moffett, preparing gems in the kitchen taught me to create beautiful ornaments with my words. I've always felt the love from the process of inscription. Surely, this love I speak of went into the food my grandmother cooked. It smelled, looked, and tasted so scrumptious. She would take her time and move about the kitchen with a particular flare, certainty, a rhythm that spoke volumes to what was being created. I've always wanted my writing to have this same effect: a particular flame, aroma, a delectable taste of honesty that connected the experience to the work, a recycling of all that I have learned from life's oven.

Thus my moniker, Food4Thot! It is an ode to my grandparents, parents, uncles, aunties, teachers, and all the colorful conversations I have overheard throughout the years while ear hustling, peeping game, poking my nose in grown folks' business, observing, and becoming a student of poetry, art, and expression.

The body of work that's presented in this manuscript is an immense expression of many different temperatures of written, raw, and cooked cuisines for the mind, body, and spirit. These palatable poems, prose, and stories have been prepped with loving hands and pure intentions. I offer them for you to taste, receive, and enjoy. I've come to learn not to over- or under-cook the food, and that food should serve as a means for strength, affording the receiver the capacity to go out and get more victuals.

Food is also the remedy for malnutrition, the medicine to guard against daily attacks on our being. When we are fed, our physiology vibrates on a higher level, allowing provisions to come in and settle hunger, desperation, and lack, as it relates to our daily existence.

It is my pleasure to be your host, waiter, cook, chef, and edutainment at this royal feast. Royalty is in our bloodline, so it is our birthright. The sooner we inner-stand this, the healthier we will be as a being, a family, a community, a society, and world at large.

I lovingly present to you
words dipped in liberation—
sure to set you free!
truth for the youth,
in this world of treachery.
I've been reserved in this poetry realm,
so you haven't heard the best of me.
The rest of me,
is in the recipe,
I must serve to the mentally famished.
Sit back, relax, and enjoy these...
Psychological sandwiches...
Served by yours truly...

I got a buffet of flows—
that will tantalize your intellect.
Causing intriguing dialect,
that will leave your brain wet,
for this cerebral hors d'oeuvre...

prepared by:

Food4Thot

333

Appetizers

-Birth, Education, Sankofa-

"From little date seeds, great things are born."

- Namibian Proverb

Arrival

Induced myself,
ready to come,
dressed in ancestral fluids.
Squatting upside down—
Afrakan style in the eye of her soft.
Lindy Hopping to ovarian music,
scribing Watts-Latin—
on womb walls to recall...

 I once was here...

birthed into forget me knots.
breastfed amnesia of God consciousness,
consecrated memories—
defecated into oblivion.
reptilian of a boy—
negotiating fire for water—
in a one-bedroom galaxy,
where dreams came in whisky bottles and
greatness gambled for rent.

Craps...
Bet-back
Apologize
Seven out tha door

I'm here...

Offspring's Vantage

toss and turn
in this micro universe
hearing a voice of familiar
baritone pitch
yearning to see this face
eyes
like mine   slanted
provider
protector   like me
this
must be Pops'
royal bloodline
that I give thanks for
my lineage expands
my heart
 in physical form

You From

Melanin molecules
Pineal intelligence
Hidden legacy
Cosmological substances

Plasma physics
Pyramid builders
Dogon sorority
Astrological superiority

Dynasty shapers
Shapeless shadow
Reflecting invisibility
Memphite theologies
Maat principles
Ptah utterances
Kings/ Queens
Indentured servants

You from

Olmec Thot
Chumash dynamism
Tribes of warriors
Sold off by your own people.
Slaves of psychopaths
Injustice overthrowers
Sojourners
Harriets
Toussaint L'Ouvertures.

Nat Turner's bravado
Douglas's narratives
Bleeding Ms. Wheatley's and Mr. Dunbar's ink

God's divine gene pool
Twa-Indian-Moors
Koori-Goori-Noongar,
The rich, the poor

Never forget where you come from...

Garveyism
Du Bois' wisdom
King's dream
Malcolm's-isms
Big Mommas
Big Pops
Tulsa-Durham-Harlem-Watts

You come from you...
Never forget...

You come from you.

Shallow Education

the system's feeding our children—
sour apples and propaganda,
through invisible Krazy Straws...
what's taught is random,
useless information
keeping our children
in-formation at all times

quality sacrificed for quantity
resulting in academic inflation
devaluation of knowledge
turning intellectual ambition into exhaustion
bright minds into dim domes
in effort to be multicultural and eclectic
class curricula
superficial
disorganized
and don't express from a global viewpoint
compartmentalized pieces of an artificial meal
students leaving unfulfilled
famished
looking for cheap thrills
through herb, meth, and X pills
to replace the emptiness
of this lackluster educational structure

history books
are filled with...
deliberately misleading inaccuracies
distortions
for the sake of corporate gain and political correctness
ineffectiveness plagues this young generation

I thought
the purpose of education
was to make one an independent,
competent thinker
truth be told,
many of us don't care,
public schools for most is an unpaid daycare

Can we get real up in here?

college is no different
remember!
education is BIG business!!!!

current conditions of total student loan debts
trumps one trillion dollars in America
Hysteria?
an understatement
so I'm pounding pavements
to liberate students from economical enslavement...
because shallow education
feeds our children sour apples and propaganda
through invisible Krazy Straws...
what's crazy, is that it tastes good...
but leaves our children on pause with infinite lockjaws!!!!
unable to articulate that they are hurting
and college isn't working...

what's taught is random, useless, and meaningless
information
keeping our children, in-formation at all times...

In Formation

325 AD.
Constantine summons
300 priests & bishops
to switch up The Good Book
extracting our black popes and pharaohs
replacing them with other faces
races instead of cultures
divided humanity and spawned vultures
do your research, young brethren
no soliciting my soul
not interested in what you're selling
atop the mountain, yelling
"Nooooooooo…
it's time for organized religion to let my people
Gooooooooooo!"

Cuz home has been taken
it's time to free our domes
and detach from the matrix
sacred thoughts will take us to places
where papyrus scripts hold combinations
to eternity's vault
we fought for too long
to settle for desecrated stories
that were robbed from Mother Afraka's womb
from insufficient, pigmented characters
characterizing God outside of us
God's inside of us
must I keep reminding us?
I will if I keep finding us
stuck! In formation!

Crazy is conforming to this illusion
delusion of grandeur

viewed through lower frequencies
creatures of idiosyncrasies
that bi-polar on credit
and on Black Friday
sell it back to our multiple personalities
creating a poor inner core
so we pawn morals and integrity
for paper notes with slavemasters on them
then cop whips, chains, and trees and hang ourselves
reincarnated as them
now you can blame yourself
for not activating the divine in you
you and the divine are one
must I keep reminding you?
I will if I keep finding you
Stuck... In... formation!

Sequoia

I'm here,
here I stand
still standing
after all these years
I see everything that happens 'round me
smoke clears briefly
casualties litter terrain,
blood drips through concrete
fertilizing roots
sprouting siblings
out of Mother's scalp

my nature is to grow,
stand strong and live long...

I am tree,
and I too
been you before
and to be free
is to be me

If the Shoe Fits

we, us, now, can't
will not listen to your garbage truck of a mouth—
unload ugly into the streets of our joy anymore.
Any more of your disregard for loving vibes—
will leave me no other choice than to...

I am open to remain closed to...
trash on Sundays,
gossip on Tuesdays,
hate on Fridays,
slander at breakfast.
two days of not hearing your voice allows—
flowers to bloom through concrete.
trees stretch to the sun when you are silent,
the universe can do without you,
your revulsion contaminates from the inside out.
this is a warning shot,
the next will be aimed at your temple,
it's simple,
cease and desist
or get snuffed and destroyed...

To whom it may concern...

If the shoe fits...

Poetry

Yellow
Yelling rays of sunlight in night's black
Wind chiming air in direction of purpose
Purposely removing distractions
Fire to sage
Smudging the stink out of the moment
Volcanic eruption via oral cavity
Represents the gravity of words, that—
Orange their blue through facades of courage
Aqua, waving waves of brilliance
When dark reveals eyelids instead of pupils
I be pupil to this cosmic order
Open to give without expectations
The freedom in this place of "stretch"
Keeps me coming back for more...
Studying creation
In awe of its unfolding
Smiling...
Giving thanks—
For the process that has all manifested in my head
It's time to put pen to paper
Mating blood with nature
Procreation of scribes
Carving excessiveness from body
Molding form from thots
Push, push, push...

A poem is born.

Forward Ever

Weeds
Grown between daisies
Releasing parallel redemption
Fighting stance...
Sunday's nectar
Picked by Monday's labor regrets
Given to child
Who has not seen a garden in real time
Nature's midwifery of angels
Guarding adolescent
Predator advancements of shhh "Don't tell no one."

Forward we must go...

Into clutter
Shaping raggedy shacks in memory sunset
Of a Ghanaian Wednesday morning
Witnessing tears form reflection of twisted smiles
Unable to tell the difference between hurt & regret
Love & war
Backwards and forward...

Forward we must go...

Into mental shifts of attacks
Left on the battlefield
To Molotov thoughts of surrender
Fighting for future generations' lost imprints

Forward ever, backwards never!

Natural Pearl

radiant iridescence
reflecting hues of splendor,
sovereignty vibrating from Nile's ripple,
a glorious oyster,
washed upon shore—
shamans pray blizzards—
out of days gray.

She pearly, grown and girly...
searching for spirituality in pariahs—
stars in the dots of leopards,
startling presence—
bids blessings to all—
that's in her universe...

You and I verses—
all challenges in her way,
we honor this magic woman,
natural pearl...
bending worlds to overlap beauty...
girls learned by gazing at her movements,
head gestures,
sit like this,
speak like that,
love yourself—
as she does.

Pillows pick fights for her attention...
so she rest on clouds—
hovering over legacy—
woven in matriarch's crochet...
she know some thangs
been thru some thangs
and shares her healing with the world...

She be S. Pearl...
Sharp,
shrewd,
a creative midwife to lost souls,
deciphering gibberish in silence...
mediating disharmony into synchronicity
hurt into healing
numbness into feeling...
touching
seeing
tasting
hearing
we now listen different when she speaks,
sit, cross our legs Indian-style—
when she teaches pearlology...
the process of nature's oysters—
hatching divinity into pearls infinity...
smooth,
fine,
rare,
radiant

She pearly, grown and girly...
searching for spirituality in pariahs—
stars in the dots of leopards,
startling presence—
bids blessings to all—
that's in her universe...

Stage Left

Float in upside down
Behind the earth
In front of the sun
Wormhole-hopping with ancestral beings...
Turban wrapped like monks,
Moors, Buddha, Yeshua, Nubia,
Shaman, sage, a Gnostic gangsta!!!
Ghost-riding a magic carpet down the Nile—
Infectious smile
Symbolizes
I see God in you!
Trusting you see it!
The moon reflects my perfect imperfections
Cigarettes and whisky
Used to smudge & libate my childhood's aura
Young pop-locking disciple of Watts
Side-stepping boobie traps
Saving cats caught in the tree of life
Painting, writing, creating the ummph!!!
In this moment...
Reversing the curse
Hook-sliding my tribe into a new direction
Pay attention, bro-bro,
I been here b4!!!
You blink, you'll miss it!!!
I've loved, lost,
Lived, given, shared, hugged, fought
Misplaced, found
Smiled, frowned
Shot
Been shot at
Transitioned, transformed
A God whisper into a shout!
... And in my quiet, I'm reminded,

My love will last forever...
As I cartwheel black & white into colors
Flip-flop inside-out myself
So you can see how I feel...
Extremely safe
In this new place of vulnerability...
Exuding all that is blessed these days...
Bad intentions can't live in this moment's glory
Helper, complement, asset,
When assisting with conundrums...
Kind-heartedness
Not to be taken for weakness
Problem solver
Still can break down a revolver
While wheeling with one hand...
Bunny-hopping over quicksand
On a Beach Cruiser
No kickstand
Turn it upside down
When I stroll...
Ya underdig?
Who am I?
Voice for the voiceless
Help for the helpless
Hope for the hopeless
Light for the lightless
Remember me
As a deep, permanent purple
Boy's body ascending into man
While slow-dancing with Melanie's forever...
God kissed thru a snaggletoothed organ
On a Watts back porch
Underneath a loquat tree...
Racing ice-cream sticks on the curb...
After a summer water-hydrant party!!!
Who am I?

Your guess is just as good as mine!

Super Food

-Life, Love, Legacy-

"The most important question in the world is, 'Why is the child crying?'"

-Alice Walker

5th Dimension

September 24th her way into my almanac
the moon glowed ultra indigo violet like...
tilting Libra scales of imbalance into JJ
prayed for the day a stork would deliver
a daughter of a blessing onto a Watts teenage
Jordan bulldog that was off the leash!
when the fog settled
she appeared
heaven in the form of a baby girl
the world's twirl would never be the same...
Jasharra Monique was the first to hold my soul!

Fourth of July, big-bang of a lifetime
blue seas parted
to tsunami a Cancer that wasn't malignant
vowed to assist in the bloom of an angel—
that became the air beneath my broken wings,
Daddy's princess Shai
knows at the end of days her voice will be the sage
that cleanses the portal for ascension
her birth created Amenta
heaven in Earth's dimension
Oshai Ashley was the second to hold my soul!

7-day theory
17 blessings manifested
94 ways to say I love you...
seven seventeen ninety four
a prince was born at St. Francis
split image of self
Man-Man, as he was called, has morphed—
into a young man of distinction
the glue that sticks families together
his half has not been told, pure heart of gold!
Denzell Otis was the third to hold my soul!!

Father's Day came with a special delivery
18th of June, 'round noon the earth quaked
to release a Gemini / Him and I ... inseparable!
his prodigy reminds me of the best parts of me
the past in the present—
Sankofa, reincarnated possibility
he holds the torch of artistry
partially the future of poetry
he's the golden child to me—
that the world will one day flock to see in droves...
Otis Derrell was the fourth to hold my soul!!!

She Sagittarius, her intro on the eve of giving thanks
just when I thot the family would lateral
her perpendicular announced...
The Most High is not done with this tribe...
I cried gratitude eleven ways through twenty-six blessings
two thousand & fourteen reasons to thank God for this season
a fortune of ecstasy eclipsed into the best of me
earth, moon, stars aligned in sublime order
the daughter of a goddess
spiritually connecting siblings via derivatives of the whole...
Love-Shari Iiona was the fifth to hold my soul!!!

Give Thanks

Met her in a daydream
Dreaming daylight into my nightmares
Sprinkling pixie dust onto the pages of our lineage
Aligning historical accounts of parallels
Destined to interlock like locs
In perfect harmony
Harmonizing liberation songs
Libation pours when she speaks
Dolphins dance when she walks
They flip to her switch
I envied her lip gloss
Glossary can't describe words I feel
Unfamiliar bliss jolts to my chakra
She climaxes me

WITHOUT SEX!

I give thanks for her...

Medicine woman
Rose petals litter her path
Cities build from her imagination
Generations of wisdom beneath her tongue
When she sneezes
Blessings come
You're blessed to be in her vapors
I give thanks for her...

Agave nectar taste
Hands show infinity
While embracing her creativity
She became my mission
I wouldn't stop until accomplished
Planting seeds by whispering

Ancient insights in my ear
My stomach growled at her presence
Marveling at her vigor
I knew she was a rarity
Clarity came via candid dialogue
In which we exchanged
Secrets for garments
Until we stood exposed in our bareness
Nectar running down our minds
We've never been this wet
And we've yet to touch each other
Our spirits Cha-Cha from across the room
Her physical bloomed like daffodils in the summer
She's ripe!
Like falling off the vine
So I nibble on her inner thigh
Sending shock waves up her spine
Blowing on her pearls
Had her speaking in tongue
And chanting in Swahili
Her Kuma
Was throbbing for my Jingillalee
I stand erect like pyramid
She's the earth
I'm the sun
The moon is our balance
Together we procreate
On Afrakan soil
So our seeds will always know their roots…

I give thanks for her

For her

I give thanks!

333 Seconds

and still...
I'm missing you.
Wishing you
into clones
so I can be with you
when I'm alone
on the road
and need a hug
and you're home
with our blessed Love.

Doves know my pain
they fly circle hearts 'round your name
fluttering thoughts of you.
On stages, smiling from
ear to ear from thoughts of you.
Whenever I see lovely sceneries,
I picture you, in the scenes with me, HD.
Thoughts of you are driving me crazy,
In a good way, my Love.

You are my altar
that I kneel in front of.
After the day has torn a brother down
you are my medicine
that I heal in front of...
I now know I'm infatuated
with making you feel appreciated, my Love.
These feelings are segregated
for you only! My Love.
Shucks, if profanity meant something,
I would probably cuss...
for every time a couple got frustrated with

trying to compare themselves to us.
We be a whole 'notha type of one,
our kingdom has come,
on Earth as it is in Heaven.
Eleven 26th her way into our forever,
so when we're together
it means something different now.
Withdrawals
when I'm not with you now.
I even miss you when I'm with you now.
How blessed I am,
to find my heart walking around
in you now.

It's now been
333 seconds…
and still…
I'm
missing
you!

NOW!!!

Her, Me, We

we began, before we begun
two-stepped into one...
reflecting a triple light

penda birds...
tweeting a tweet
Twitter can't twit
shoot, we go back like...
Food and Socks
moon rocks & dinosaurs
why else would purple dolphins
flip-flop over Gerbera daisies in my rest
plucking heart strings in trumpet's song
echoing her voice in Simone's tone...
Shabaka Stone...
decoding the language of blue and yellow
Ethiopian parrots
repeating a green agape shairi back and forth
on the 1st of September,
written in galaxy scribble
on a Watts project brick....
stuffed in 12-inch woofer boxes
playing Debra Laws's "Very Special"
backwards in Swahili
every time a 6-tray Chevy hit the switch!

whatcha know 'bout us?   bwooooooooy.

synchronized inhales,
held until hell freezes over
we be all over each other like all *over* each other...
(sigh)...
exhaling simultaneous
Blessed Vibrations

lavender, hibiscus,
peppermint breath
blew into whole
spirit gardens of legacy seeds
sprouting our next us
into star dust
forming nuptials
twisted with sage spray...
noting infinity into a love lock
soaked in Still Waters
dipped in a coco-mango body butter
that carries
SWEET memories of November 7th,
forever 3 hours, 33 minutes, trapped and aged
under chipped fingernails
that show...

good moments,
good loving,
good living,
good mornings,
good days,
good nights...

GOOD GOD!!!

her, me, we...
we began before we begun

whatcha'll know 'bout that?

We Be Chosen

when we are quiet
portals open
exactly as envisioned
in visions of blessedness
Love envelopes all
releasing uneasiness
for life's distractions

in this now
their breath
be background music
mother-daughter giggles
a symphony of harmonies
heartbeat within heartbeat
synchronized with pulse
souls courting spirit…
into divine gene pool
illuminating birth canal

there she is…

best part of me
us
we
she
birthing eternity

a bridal chamber of doulas
assist to birth tomorrows
into always
in always
all ways are
lead back to our always
ways are all connected

in this circle of tribe
lineage, legacy
leg I see in ultra
sam sung Hathaway
voice away
as we sit on dock's bay...
transcending time
space/moments/distractions
contractions/release

there she is...
there she is...
best part of me
us
we
she
birthing eternity
wisdom personified
earth, moon, stars...
seen her
before I saw her
sawed flaws
fell off to birth amenta
angels
renegotiate the atmosphere
for her arrival
saw her before I seen
her
see-sawed into balance
maat—
vivid
HD
melanie's melody
into me
mel & me
joined to birth she
we be one in three
three in one

contract
expand
release

there she is
there she is

best part of me
us
we
she
birthing eternity

there she is...

Love

Barbara

a special kind of grace
that can walk through a lie in six-inch pumps
while hitching a ride with stone-cold killas
flame of confidence
that announces the queen has arrived
strange eyes glued to silhouette
baffled onlookers think...
"god took her time with this one!"
dark, fine, rare, intelligent superwoman
who counted cards in her sleep to awake
and hit black-jack every time
how does she stand through seizures
dance between nervous breakdowns
cha-cha while taking six different medications
smiling through pain
offering her last cent to help someone else...?
this magician of a woman
remembers
finding her mother deceased
with self-inflicted
gunshot wound to the head
and a suicide note that read...
something I can't articulate
words my pen can't write
fingers can't type
this black teen
left to figure it out by her lonesome
and yes   she did   she did
...she has always exuded
a special type of grace
that suggests ...
god   took her time with this one!

Father Like Sun

Food—   Afrakan Baba's
Offspring off Eastside wisdom
Navigating blocks
Shielding our children
From red beams
Pointed at vertebrates
Sprinkling
Ancestors'
Holy waters
On the foreheads
Of suns & daughters
Decreasing the murder rate

Future—   We be
Children of warrior parents
Battle scars mark our bodies
Like tattoos
From a fight
We didn't choose
But was born into
We are blessed
With the heart of the panthers
Soul of the ancestors
So we can't lose...
We can't lose!

Cosmic Balance

Milele usawa
tunaishi katika nyakati kati ya pumzi
kinga ya chini ya maji
kutafakari Zulu utulivu
kushikana mikono
ikitoa nje ya mawazo obiti
katika etha
mbinguni kuwa kama sisi

Translation:

Eternal balance
we live in moments between breath
breathing under water
meditating Zulu stillness
holding hands
releasing out-of-orbit thoughts
in ethers
heaven be like us

Purple Analysis

Divinity
Exuding favor
Inside of flowers' bloom
Pollinating nature's moist
Quenched in a universal cloak of harmony
Inebriated from pure intentions
Rippling ocean of chest
Quaking aftershocks of blessedness

Time's absent
In this moment's glance
Where moon smiles atop newborns tender
In wink of mother's lashes

We live here
Inside of there
Over yonder
Exploring lessons
Passed down from Big Momma's
"Be careful wishes"

Dishes done … check!
Clothes washed … check!
Clean undergarments … check!
Never know what might occur

I hear you, Nana
I do remember how snuff smells
Truth sounds
Leftover cake icing 'round bowl onto adolescent fingertips
I can taste it…

Fear doesn't exist in these purple memories!!!

Black Spirit

I penda her neyusi roho
Rhooing thru ancient baharis
To capsize on her chi

Shaman bow on magic carpet
Hovering over projects
Covering offspring with sacred sage mist

Chanting "Veggie" Latin
Aboriginal Eastside
Bebop tongue

Mystery potion
Oozing from genie bottle
Forming shadow of familiar

Lovers rock locked empress
Appeared picking papayas
On sovereign scalp

Spirit talking with trees/
Ye queen of light—
Crafting copper
Into ankh antennas
Modest dose of
Perpetuity in stare

Black spirit, I see you

I see you, black spirit.

November Whispers

She hums
In ears of guardian ancestors
Tamu sentiments
Covered in lavender jazz
Her jaded efforts
Shift paradigms
In dimensions reserved for few
On my behalf she represents...
Topaz
Hues of sunset
Speckled over
Purple and sky blue
Our penda
The basis
For nation's conflict resolutions
Atrocities forgiven
From her tea remedies...
Find our story
Where stars align
Planets Cha-Cha

Galaxies kiss

Geb has prepared me
To receive her all
Snout open
Turmeric nostrils
Lilac aroma coexists with frankincense
In my dreams
Scriptures wake me in falsetto
Serenading sacred hymns
Of our anecdote...

Rain Woman

Remembering dates
Calendars have yet to record
Jig-sawing Delanta from seizures
Shaking backwards into the womb of forget

Autumn falls harder
When police tape is wrapped 'round
Childhood glance
Winstons
Folgers
Bookie joints
Warped already distorted reality
Third grade
Ms. Wysoki's class
Undergarments
Du-rag
Large piece of leather
The chase ensued
I made it to the rest

Spent ten years
Sticking spoons down her throat
They said she would choke
Until sunset welcomes her to ancestors' vantage
Not now
She's my boogeyman slayer
Melting nightmares into smoothies
She's my super shero
My momma
Barbara—

The Rain Woman

Pops

Round 1

Young brain
Sharp, strong, witty—
Figuring out problems
That haven't occurred, while wheeling
On a Harley with David and sun
A go-getter, getting all necessities for his tribe

Round 2

Bobbing and weaving
Dancing with the energy of a volcano
Black tornado spinning into mortgage paid
Full stomachs, manly duties done

Round 3, 4, 5, 6, 7

A breeze
Swinging on doubt
Knocking out complacency
Arm wrestling with monsters
Shooting the boogeyman dead
For showing up unannounced

Round 8

Men contract this 50% more than women
50,000 Americans are diagnosed each year
It can't happen to Superman
He feels a shake
Mild to massive in the winter
Massive to uncontrollable in the summer
There's no cure…

Round 9

By the time it's diagnosed
50-80% of dopamine neurons have died—
Leaving it nearly impossible to catch at an early stage
Alzheimer's cousin
Progressive neurodegenerative
Motor system disorder

Round 10

Drugs, drugs, drugs, and more drugs
L-Dopa, carbidopa, levodopa
All convert into dopamine in the brain
Side effects: muscle spasms, memory loss, sleep disorder
Hallucinations...

Round 11

Get out of his head; get out of his head
They're playing tetherball in his head—
Get out of his head; get out of his head

Round 12

 Winner by unanimous decision
And still undisputed father-weight champion of the world...

Otis "The Harley Man" Perry!

My dad.

Community

Sunset
Fire
Tree
Elder
Youth
You
Love
We chant hymns
Unison
Releasing toxins through weep
Resting
Holding
Listening
Blessing
Welcoming new arrivals to courtyard
Drum
Voices
Eyes
Coughs
Sneezes
Sage
Children, children, children
Babies bless you
Food preparation
Dance
Stomp
Rain
Rain
Life
We are thinking
Sharing
Breathing life
Life

Life
Babies
You with child?
No child?
Sure, you have child...
Our children are our children
Hours pass
Seconds
Happy
Games
Live alive
We are communing
Community
Commune
Tea
Tea
Community
Let's commune
Over a cup of tea...

Entrees

-Loyalty, Truth, Our-Story-

"You have to learn to get up from the table when love is no longer being served."

-Nina Simone

Royal Feast

Dawn breaks
when Cherry's trumpet
reverberates thru Mud Town
sounds of Mingus strumming cello—
upside-down bidding—
a primordial echo
a cosmic "Arkestra,"
orchestrated by Tapscott's key strokes
Higgins's kick drum
Collette's saxophone moans
summonsing all
Mother Watts's children home...

Come one, come all...
Ye gods are having a ball!
Let us pray, eat, and dance bold—
To the rhythm of our souls...

Been mixing
these ol' recipes
for centuries
this mystic brew
cosmic stew
these intergalactic provisions—
prepared with love to heal—
internal incisions—
thru paternal visions...
breastfed from Mother Barbara's soul ... all natural
served lukewarm in the cold...
my life's been a two-fold menu—
written in arthritic longhand over—
a smoking scroll—
of psychological formulas
overindulgence

may cause an overdose
must warn ya!

Cuz this right here...

be that real talk Crock-Pot liquor
balsamic vinegar juke joint hot sauce kicker
cross-eyed black-eyed peas
and dirty taters mashed
'tween corn and tomatoes
paid fo' in gold and pesos
so they know
Afraka and Mexico go back
like Kush and Olmec—
seeds in fertile grounds...
frowns turn upside down
when witnessing the way harvest grows...
...and day blows royalty thru McNeely's tenor
Wanda Colman's "Be Out of Heaven by Sundown, Niggah"
announces it's time for dinner...

Come one, come all...
Ye gods are having a ball!
Let us pray, eat, and dance bold—
To the rhythm of our souls...
It's time to feast...

Fellowship—
while Dr. King—
brews up the melanin trip
opening the doorway to Amenta
loose-leaf teas reversing—
the effects of dementia...
remember? remember?
we remember now!
YES!!!

We remember...
Babas, Yayas
rocking halos titled east
Nguzu Zaba
Karamu
Kwanzaa
welcome to this Royal Feast
of unrehearsed char-broiled verses
dispersed throughout the universe
placed royally on an extended banquet table—
suspended in the galaxy—
scribed in the stars
covered with food for the mind—
body and spirit from Earth to Mars—
Neptune to Sun
Where there's more than enough for everyone...
It's time to feast!

Come one, come all...
Ye gods are having a ball!
Let us pray, eat, and dance bold—
To the rhythm of our souls...

Partaking in a cerebral collard-green mixture
hand-churned, butternut squashed—
come get you some of these holy 'hood scriptures
black-power beans, lightly seasoned—
over yellow street rice, Eastside lettuce
agave-glazed mental alfalfa sprouts
first fruits just ripe!

Come one, come all...
Ye gods are having a ball...
"Is it not written in your law,
I said you are gods?"
John 10:34, Yeshua spoke!
The tribe listened...

Listen!

It's time to pray, eat, and dance—
in the spirit of forgiveness...

Bring your ugly, infidelity
betrayal, mistakes, regrets
your...
should've
would've
could've
done this and that better... I BET!
yo' momma did not love you
daddy never hugged you
bring it / bring it / bring it—
your insecurities, lies, fears

To the feast of all saints
shamans, Gnostic gangstas
seers, prophets, soothsayers,
oracles, psychics, clairvoyants
hustlers and flamboyant preachers
students, gurus, and grand-master teachers...

Come one, come all...
Ye gods are having a ball!
Let us pray, eat, and dance bold—
To the rhythm of our souls...

Creating a magnificent healing
reversing the curse of the plague
families fed
the young will rise from the walking dead
to spearhead the next revolution
food is the remedy

the spirit is the solution
We royal 'round these parts...
I proclaim with a smile...
The band's playing
elders praying
children playing
poets are spraying—
truth-sayings over the crowd.

Come one, come all...
Ye gods are having a ball!
Let us pray, eat, and dance bold—
To the rhythm of our souls...
Allowing our spirits to speak –
Welcome to this Royal Feast!

Bon Appétit...

"I am a Negro: Black as the night is black, Black like the depths of my Africa."

-Langston Hughes

The Darker Brother

I, too, sing America
I be charcoal coco-latte
Chanting
Rise up, ye mighty people
Rise up, ye mighty race

I am Negro
A dream variant of simplicity
Carved creative marble-breasted
Cracked leather etched into chalk lungs
Coughing a weary blues
I sneeze renaissance
And bless haiku

I be Ptah
Fashioning the Universe
Through harmonics and thought
Medu Neter chiseled in me chest plate
Checkmate in three
Me now know why the caged bird sings
So me drink suffering
And piss triumph

I am burnt cork
Greased paint
Spread like chocolate bar
Slice of melon rind

I be melanin
Nyuesi
Pigmented to the third power
The antithesis of pale

I am the Watts Prophets
Rappin' Black in a White World
The Last Poets
Proclaiming *This Is Madness*

I am Harlem
"A Dream Deferred"
"They send me to eat in the kitchen
when company comes"

I be Watts
Conceptions and misconceptions
Blacks Arts Movement
Blues People
Negro Music in White America

I am *The Souls of Black Folk*
The sage of Anacostia
"Genius Child"
"Busy sharpening my oyster knife"
Doctoring Toomers cut by Cane

I be *Black Magic*
Word sorcerer
360 Degrees of Blackness Coming at You
Black Feeling
Black thought
Black Talk
Re: Creation
My House
The Women and the Men
Cotton Candy on a Rainy Day
And *Those Who Ride the Night Winds*

I am sorrow
Sung thru lost vernacular
Spilled on Dixie's breast

Whipped with black belts
Bleeding solitary tears for glory

I am "A Negro Love Song"
A "Little Brown Baby"
"The Corn-Stalk Fiddle"
"The Haunted Oak"
"Ships That Pass in the Night"

I am an invisible
Shouting words felt but never heard
Muffled
Lips ostracized my nerves
Where in the kitchen
I eat
I laugh
And I grow
Stronger for the day, to tell the world
How it feels to be colored me...

I am
Marcus Garvey
Langston Hughes
W.E.B. Du Bois
The Watts Prophets
The Last Poets
Amiri Baraka
Sonia Sanchez
Nikki Giovanni
Wanda Coleman
Jayne Cortez
Paul Laurence Dunbar
John Blak
Lukuma Kwa Luja
a.k.a Food4Thot! I am ... The Darker Brother

and... I, too, sing AMERICA!

"In the sense that I also try to reflect the fullness of the black experience, I'm very much a jazz poet."

-Jayne Cortez

Old School

Old School
Like five on da black-hand side
Throwback like forty fives & 8-tracks
They den' played me on jukeboxes
At juke joints
Where old-timers chewed snuff
Shot pool
Stayed on point
Like a pair of Stacys
Peeping out the bottom of some bell bottoms

I often poly with Esther
With my bee-bop tilted
George Clinton & the Watts Prophets
Kept me lifted
I'm really so gifted
With this gift of gab
That I use to uplift and inspire
I'm
Earth
Wind
Fire
Wrapped in Kente cloth
Tap-dancing in shell toes
To the rhythm of soul
I crochet my flow
So that I reap what I sow
I get deep with these sea-scrolls
That's delivered
From a Watts Pee-Chee Folder
I'm colder than your coldest winter
In December
I'm that raggedy black & white T.V.
With aluminum foil on my antennas...

On June 12th, 2009
I did not convert to the converter box
To let the government watch me
Me rather watch
Dr. John Henrik Clarke
Malcolm X
Expose the government on VHS
We made less
'Cause we loved rest
But my mother made miracles
In the kitchen feeding a family of 10
With one chicken
And a loaf of Wonder's best
I told her I was still hungry
She would say…
"Imagine the rest."
Grabbing my chest
Inhaling secondhand smoke at its best
Tobacco companies said it was cool to smoke Cools
And entertain Virginia's Slim dress
Didn't tell us it will leave lumps on our Queens' breast
Pumps for our Kings' chest
To resuscitate life

I'm from the era where drive-bys didn't exist
You had to get out in the streets and fight
Whipped butt
Or get your butt whipped
But we both woke up the next day
Playing throw'em-up tackle
In the middle of the streets
With a boom box beating on our shoulders
"It's like a jungle sometimes; it makes me wonder
How I keep from going under"
Grandmaster Flash & Melle Mel
No cell phone
Page me
911 if it's urgent

When I was a child, we bathed in dish detergent
Don't let the water out
Your brother must use it...
My mother would lose it
When she saw me blowing up the pink bag
On the back of the bathroom door
I was just trying to put it under water
To make bubbles
But it broke my heart when I found out
What she used that for!!!!!

I still can taste vinegar to this day!!!!

I'm Old School
Like five on the black-hand side
I'm throwback like forty fives & 8-tracks...

Old School!!!

"Every hallelujah holds
A praise for how we got over
How our souls look back and wonder."

-Jaha Zainabu

Me Be Poet

Poet me be
Pen-toting propaganda portal opener
Opening channels to effect change
Changing post-slavery effects
With this lyrical lynch Willie-ism
That's been brewing in me gut for over 4,000 years
Ancestors' tea pot been screaming
Redemption song
While blood tears
Runneth over to a river
That's saturated in oil spills

I ... Food4Thot
Earnestly vow
To write words
That wrap 'round injustices
Squeeze till life pop out
Love takes precedence
Just as this
Moment has eternal implications
Implicating...
We are who we've been waiting for!

On that note
I shall grip pen tight
Write!!!
Till Emmett Till's plasma seeps
Regurgitating Oscar Grant's
regards for the system
Swing like Latasha Harlins
to the head of the power structure
Deandre Brunston middle finger
to the consequences
Compliments of this Field Poet!!!

Love for the rod
Balance for me staff
Me be the voice of the streets
That's uniquely equipped
To speak on her behalf
Cuz half of me
Still in the streets

While they shucking and jiving on social network
Me networking with unsocial soldiers
To deliver this message to the culprits
Nowadays
Most pimps wear halos
And stand behind pulpits
Posing for nude flicks

CLICK!!!

Sending them to choir boys
Don't be quiet boy
Or become that man's boy toy
Toys are for boys, MAAAAAN!!!
Liquor stores on every corner
Keep us in a trance
Unable to tap into the God inside of us
So we search outside of us
For a God that we wouldn't know
If she breastfed us daily…

Ancient

Medu Neter scribe
In our DNA
A.N.D. we rock
Like rock & roll
Before they got hold to it
It, too, come from us
Us come from way back
Djembe sound
Congo rhythm
Rhythm's us
Us rhythm
We HOT!
Hot like
Soul sistas
In the summertime
Partying in the basement
Doing the Funky Chicken in hot pants
Hot like Big Momma's pots & pans
Hot like fish grease
In black skillet
Me black like skillet
Blue black
Black-blue they eye
For disrespecting my queen
Black man, we king like Akhenaten
Old-school T-Bird stopping
Down Capitol Hill
Shouting F%#K the Senate bill
We still searching for justice for
Oscar Grant
Michael Brown
And Emmett Till
And all unnamed casualties
That ever fell victim
To America's psychopathic mentality

We pour libation
And say...
ASÈ

Agents
We see you making deals with the enemy
Plotting to cause the end of me
That will never be
Jab him in the throat
And go to whooping on him like Ali
Baba
Keep 40 thieves behind me
On the blocks of Watts teaching ancient history
To the lost flock
Is where you're bound to find me
Amongst the less fortunate and the grimy
Look for me
Like M dot. Garvey
In the heart of the whirlwind
We ain't never scared
When those pistols go to popping like popcorn
Most revolutionary cats ain't never there
Yet, they come around after someone gets killed
With fists in the air, hollering revolution
If Malcolm
Nat Turner
And Garvey were alive
They would say to stop marching and start shooting
'Cause the war out here
We are losing
By killing each other
The system is killing us too
The revolution
Is broke
And needs capital
And these streets
Need to know about
Auset

Ausar
And Heru
So both sides need each other
Like old folks need soft shoes
When we see military tanks dipping up Crenshaw
What we gon' do?
Assimilate then?
Too late, my friend...
They going to murk you
Notify your next of kin
Then ship revolutionary men to concentration facilities...
I spit verbal artillery
Whether or not the people feeling me
I'm just tired of playing these cards
they been dealing me...
For way too long
'Cause me and my people are too black
And way too strong
To let this ride...
So are y'all ready to ride???
Well, you best be ready to die
'Cause the revolution might get televised
With two slugs between your eyes
Cold-case files
Swollen face can't smile
Bloated waist moves bile
Biological warfare
Katrina was by design
They been messing with the air
You betta do your research
'Cause they can make the earth shake
Blow up a country
And blame it on an earthquake!

"When you can do the common things of life in an uncommon way, you will command the attention of the world."

-George Washington Carver

Who I Be

Many miss when jewels drop
Out of the blue like huge rocks
Hues rocks...
Like Big Momma in rocking chair
Graphed quake optics
Don't the Quaker Oats man
Look like Barbara Bush
On them old-school oatmeal boxes?

That's another topic
So I'ma drop it
Cuz they're up
We're stuck
Between hick and up!
Hiccup ... excuse me
Flows just flow through me
Like Wallace Christopher
Big up, Biggie!

Hope y'all picking up what I'm puttin' down
The Most High
Places valuables in the ground

So my hope
Is for the young to get into this
Sorta like your 1st kiss
My flow's limitless
We been at this
Way before they mom dukes
Gave pops benefits

Remember this
Next time you wanna spew nonsense in my direction
my work's older than dad's foreskin complexion

No shots fired!

Just need you to remember
But in present tense
Past been past
But the present
A gift!!!

Royal presence
A prerequisite of genetics
That's in me

Although the enemy be trying to end me
My wife Melanie's melanin and me
Activates synergy
Center-chi
Vibrates my inner G
God in me
Church yell blaspheme
Blast for me
I'll blast for you
Through words that bless and bury adversaries
If you're celibate
Don't sell a bit
Until you marry yourself!
In a course
Enter course
In formed with seatbelt and helmet on
For your protection
Or crash, dummy
Don't become a crash dummy
All over some crash, dummy!

Triple entendre
Let's dibble and conjure up
A play to have us all up
On the scoreboard
Their wack offense

Got the crowd bored
Got to come harder than that
Their squad's like broke phone booths
We're kicking their quarter back

Running backwards
Running back words
Their running-back
Overheard from this huddle

No stealing this
We're living this
This gift came in stillness
With love in a cuddle...

Still in this struggle
Watts affiliate
Then split phillies with
Lawyers, dignitaries, killers, and senates
Gon' stay independent
Like witch doctors and hood dentists
We know which doctors come spiritually
recommended
From the scribes
To prescribe an elixir
And send it in a pendant
To the princess that doesn't believe
She's an ascendant of magnificent
Fancy this locket around her modest
So she won't drop it
To remain the hottest
Rather, hot is
Because she exudes HOTNESS!!!

Y'all got this?

Naw, y'all still trying to figure who I be
Well, I be Watts 1965 in 3033

'92 rebellion
Bailing 92 felons
Out of the Twin Towers' distortion
Before the abortion
Abort shun by protest
A pro tested the aftermath
Finding after the math was calculated
It didn't add up
Like Roman numerals
On the side of an Afrakan ice-cream truck
Shut the front door!!!
Miss us with the madness
Mr. & Mrs. Mad this
Royal Feast is FIRE!!!
Like 95 cowboys burning in Dallas
Mavericks with oral gymnastics
Cuban mark?
Surpassed it!!!
Mansa Musa with the Mula
Mali empire heiress
365 no days off Ferris
CALL US SIRE
And we won't stop rocking, even when we retire
I'm tired of coming down to conversate
To converse they must come higher
Chucks Converse
Got them thinking we're all-stars
Truth be told
We all are in a cosmic sixth sense
Since point six percent of what it's worth
Means only one-tenth is gonna get this
The rest...
Will just try to figure out who I be...

I told them

I BE WATTS 1965 IN 3033

OG Big Rob-In-The-Hood
Stopping the rich from robbin' the 'hood
'Cause God's in the 'hood
In a hood
And they think it's the Grim Reaper
So they run away from their blessings
And play middle man with the preacher!

I can learn from you youngins
And also teach ya!

I've sat at the feet of giants and learned scholarly science
From welders of severed thought
I'm a preserver of elder thought
My verbiage is organic like fresh carrots and asparagus
Lentils, Brussels sprouts
Aiming to make your mental muscles sprout
A tree of synchronicity
So you don't have to ask who I be...

But in case you forgot!

I BE WATTS 1965 IN 3033

"A people's relationship to their heritage is the same as the relationship of a child to its mother."

-Dr. John Henrik Clarke

Eclectic Expressions

Expressing through heartbeats
Beating hearts beat over 100,000 times a day
35,000,000 times per year
2.5 billion times in a lifetime...
In my lifetime
I express
You express
We express
Through beats of eclectic expressions

Our hearts are sound vibrations
Played from the beats
Of Mother Earth's worn fingertips
Our eclectic styles express
Diversity amongst the village
My East Afrakan wrap
Doubles as a cape
I am half man, half miraculous
All-encompassed expression
Through beats of the heart
Our heart beats
To the same energy
Beats of eclectic expressions
Expressing Afrakan rain dance
Drum circle/ blues/ jazz/ bebop/ hip hop
Ogun/ Monk/ Parker/ Mingus/ Gil Scott-Heron
The way we move
The world be staring
Glaring at our magic
Expressing rhythm
In her sway/ nature when she pray
Bass/ drum/ snare/tenor
Renders her eclectic
She's nothing less than perfect

When she goes from
Flip-flops and jumpsuits
To Manolo pumps and business suits

Beating down the runway of life
Expressing songs in her talk
Art when she walks
The masterpiece of her stance
Reflecting the universe when she dance
Ohhh ... when she dance...
Rain comes
Seasons change
Rivers flow
Crops grow again
She dances like nobody's watching
Rocking back and forth
Forth and back
From a bald head to locs
Braids to weaves
She's so eclectic
Nothing to mess with
When she weaves
Her educated vernacular
With street-common sense
Tolerance short!!!
For nonsense!!!!
Since the beginning of time
She spins and twirls the world when she winds
She beats of eclectic expression
We express through eclectic expressions
You express through eclectic expressions
The world expresses through
Beats of eclectic expression...

Flowers

How beautiful it is to be loved
It's not your birthday or anniversary
Yet and still a wonderful arrangement
Of long-stemmed roses comes for you today

As DNA drips from bouquet to your lip
The first time he called you a bit*h
You let it slide/ just in case he had slipped
Unbeknownst to you / it was the genesis
Of an abusive relationship

Revelations sprung from his tongue
Of how worthless you've become
Beating your body like a conga drum
The consecutive intakes of left hooks
Has the right side of your face numb
But it's okay/ cuz the brother got you

"Flowers Today"

At the cost of your dignity
He's literally the epitome
Of evil, posing as chivalry
Gloats in your misery
Finds peace in your defeats
We watched
How you went from alive and joyful
He reduced you to anti-social
My gullible sister/ punches to your head
Is a non-negotiable/ in whichever array they're presented
Cover girl covering black eye with make-up
Nowadays got her hating herself
This possibly may warrant psychiatric help

To replenish your power
Usually he would enter in the late-night hours
Demanding sex
The reek of liquor on his breath overwhelms the aroma
Of previously delivered flowers/ so he inflicts pain
Because he's a coward
That has to impose his will on you
If he can't control you
Eventually he's going to KILL YOU!
But nonetheless, you continue to stay
Feeling guilty for trying to leave
And besides/ he got you

"Flowers Today"

Today/ more flowers come than ever before
Friends arrive that you haven't seen
In 10 years or more
As tears scurry from their eyes
While wondering "WHY?"
As you lay beautifully nestled
In a mahogany coffin
With your neck split from ear to ear
My dear ... it's too late for you
So this message is for your peers

Abusers come in all shapes and sizes
Doctors, lawyers/ rich or poor
Many types of disguises / I suggest
You address this topic before the surprise
Because oftentimes when temperatures rise
It can lead to an unexpected demise

Blessed is the woman who realizes
Life is worth more than a bouquet
As we bow our heads and pray/ for all the
Queens that received
"Flowers Today"

Turn the Page

I write so much—
my phalanges cramp up and get charley horses
when pen strokes page
magic is made
smoking like sage
releasing all evil forces
of course this
union of me/ pen/ and pad
will be till death do us part
so there will be no divorces
navigating life's obstacle course
with a telescope planted on my third eye
griotly penetrating racism from the apex of the pyramid—
which gives me a bird's-eye—
view of what me ancestors went through
for the last four thousand years
got my heart hurting and soul in tears

Turn the page!

As I burn the stage
with generations of rage
that engraved symbols on my temple
resembling ancient hieroglyphics
translated into verbal artillery
that's discharged when I see my queens courting queens
and my kings sporting lipstick!
bearing witness to false prophets
orally ejaculating feel-good sermons—
in order to pacify our current situation
cracks the new noose
ghettos the plantation
hanging ourselves

by free-basing
and embracing a nation
that's been defacing our creation—
since Washington's administration
it's time to collectively attack this monster we facing
tracing back
to when they packed, stacked, set sail, and unplugged us—
from the Motherland
brought to another land
taught to show no love for the brotherman
we'd rather cut each others' throats and spend C-notes—
with the other man, as they stretch invisible ropes 'round—
our necks like rubber bands—
hanging us all at the same time—
flood the 'hood with guns and dope—
and charge us all with the same crime—
the blind leading the blind
got us entwined in these prevalent signs of the time…

Turn the page!

As I click, clack, cock
stand watch, ready to pop and drop the enemy
by any means necessary—
with Malcolm's intent peeping out of the window
aligning my chakras with my history
so I'm receptacle to telepathic signals
transmitted into JPEG visuals in my mind
to a time when we stood as kings & queens
not killing each other for nickels & dimes—
press rewind and find there were many throughout history—
that stood to salvage our decade's legacy
alienated, amputated, from ancient KEMET
has us prone to these inhumane complexities … it's time
to>>>

Turn the page!

Wine & Spirits

(Watts, CA)

"I Crip Walk backwards into West Afrakan rain dances."

-Food4Thot

Ease In

I ease in like wind
Cha-Cha'in sideways
In dinosaur-tip Stacy Adams roller skates
Rolling an eight out of a quarter
Convertible deuce and a quarter squats
Next to 3 pit bulls and a weight bench
Out of the backyard of Watts

Rocking a purple polyester jumpsuit
Spinning into a James Brown split
Ice pick tucked in my turban
What they hit fo'?
Tossin' glass peppermint dice
Out of a black leather cup
I'm a bad...
Motha... SHUT YO' MOUTH!!!

Fa sho shot, bro shot...

Watts Prophet
Rappin' Black in a White World

In the words of Redd Foxx
"If you catch me with a white girl...
I'm holding her for the police."

"Although the face and culture of Watts is experiencing astounding cultural changes, there are some of us still able to point out the very spot the first bomb was thrown. No plush buildings or asphalt streets can silence the screaming soil of ghettos, like Watts, soaked with the innocent blood and tears of our dead, dying, and soon-to-be-dead youth, because America's racist system refuses to protect them."

- **Richard Dedeaux**
The Watts Prophets

Wizard of Watts
(Baba Amde)

Can I have permission from an elder to speak?
"Granted."

When the student is ready
The master teacher will appear
Out of a cloud of indigo majesty
Stands the Wizard of Watts after the smoke clears...
Man, scribe, prophet, poet
Scribing in ancient hand script
Pen dipped in Mother Watts's DNA...
His resume reads like holy 'hood scriptures
Recited in Big Momma's church-hymn voice
On a bright, sunny day!!!

Queen Mother Shirley as his wisdom/guide/ sunlight
Activating nocturnal vision, allowing him to see at night!
Purple powder
Projecting blue flames
When wind blows
Tornados pause when he blinks
Quantum leaping when he thinks
As a child, he stitched angel wings together—
From cut stars left littered across the sky
Ancestors spoke
He listened in haste...
Inceptioned his way into youths' nightmares
Leaving champion Post-it notes—

To remind them of victory's sweet taste

Wizard of Watts
Watts Wizard
That has guided his flock
Through blizzards
Storms
With timeless poems
Words
Prayers
Direction
The complexion of greatness
He wears well
We ring the bell
Of valor
Honor
Homage
For Baba Amde

This is my ode
To the master teacher
For paving the way
Making a way
For me to display
This sacred art today!!!

Asè

Mother Watts #2

Wormhole
Sprouting parentless children
From vodka and rum vomit
Avatar of concrete jungle
Standing 2.12 square miles
In the belly of Lost Angels
She's tired
From rape, torture, predator advances
Oh, Mother Watts
Birthing giants that kill each other
A shell of her former self
Where I crawl and rest
From time to time
Oh, Mother Watts…
Breastfeeding a community with no milk—
And shotguns for pumps
I don't blame you
You are still standing
Feeble & strong
Short & long
Painfully calling your offspring home
We hear you
Write you
Knowing you are rejoicing from
Our reverence of this voyage
Under the supermoon
Until we come home again…

I Know These Parts #1

Get'cho butt up
Get ready for school
Was the alarm I heard every morning

Removing roaches from Sugar Smacks
To help quiet stomach rumblings
Crack pipes
Used needles
Condoms
Littered path to education
Daylight breaks
Piercing gunshot hole in wooden fence
Flowers beneath
Represent victim

Dogs bark
As tho they see evil spirits
Causing mischief
Buckets crank
But never start
Leaving room for shadetree mechanics
To worsen problems

Businessman gets blow job
In brand-new Mercedes
Hours later
Carcass of Mercedes sits on four crates

I know these parts

I Know These Parts #2

What if I told you that...
I popped a pistol before
I read my 1st book ...
Would you believe me?
Then told you that...
by the sixth grade, I shot dice,
watched crack cook,
and ran numbers all at the same time.
Would you judge me?
Then told you that...
my mother found my grandmother—
shot dead in the head before I was alive
...and Waco County Police Department
labeled it homicide.
In turn, my mother had 3 nervous breakdowns
before I turned nine...
...and I recently found out that—
my grandmother's death was a suicide.
Can you relate to that?
Helping me pick up the pieces to this puzzle,
putting together a masterpiece that will
turn tragedy into triumph...
are you up for the task?
Let's start by taking off your mask
exposing your inner secrets and scars!
Baby girl, you don't have to jump in and out of cars—
In order to master the pain of your uncle—
going in and out of you...
you too were only nine.
...And by 19 ½ she's had four abortions,
from uncles forcing themselves inside of her.
Oh, what a vicious cycle we perpetuate,
turning our noses up at the youngsters—
on the corners serving weight.

It's not his fault,
if by age 9 ½,
he knew that 9 ½ cost $4,500
and would bring back 13 ½ slightly stepped on—
so he kept on flipping it like floor exercises,
and the Beach Cruiser went to a 5 Series,
then that went up two extra sizes.
He's no longer the fat kid in G-rides,
he now taps butts,
and clanks glasses in high rises.
Till them jealous guys—
came in ski masks and with .45s
sending one of my closest guys to the Most High!!!
High most of the time to escape the matrix,
poor schools,
housing
communities—
then they send them to jail,
when they release their hatred.
What do they expect?
It's highly unlikely that the youth of today,
will sit back and wait for a county check.
They'd rather check county records,
to see if they patna got away with robbing that bank with that TEC!!!
Heck!!!
I'm just gonna give you the real,
not tripping off how it makes you feel,
cuz I still gotta hold chrome steel like stove-top,
ever since 1992 when they lit my Cadillac up like a Crock-Pot,
off 116th and Avalon—
you won't catch me napping again—
in this concrete Lebanon...
cuz I know these parts...
I know these parts well!!!

I Know These Parts #3

Dream in high definition
Awake and TiVo fairy tales
Aligning parallels with reality
Birthing clarity
Through divine assignments
Been battle tested
On these streets
Told better
Policeman catch you
With pistol
Than jackers to catch you without heat

Youngins pack heat like oven
Grind on block like bad brakes
Metal to metal
Headed for collision
Lil man's 3rd eye vision's impaired while smoking dust
Everything's in slow motion now
He can't feel face now
Car flipped over
Dead at thirteen
Mother's only child
Daddy's cracked out
His whereabouts?
Go figure!!!

Pastor see youngsters hustling
On corners and yell...
"REPENT NOW OR BURN IN HELL!!!"

Not realizing he's burning now
'Cause he's preaching
With mistress's vagina stench on tongue

Very life contradicts
What he's supposed to be standing on

We supposed to take the pastor serious???
Father, please help us...

Revolutionary man yells, "BLACK POWER!"
Power yells back, "NOT WITHOUT CAPITAL!"
Movement paralyzed in its tracks...

Tracking history through needle tracks
Up panther's arms
Only reveals dependency!
No clemency for the poor
With liquor stores
On every corner
Coroners stay busy 'round here
Bodies get dumped and found 'round here...
On a daily...
Another homicide
Retaliation makes it genocide
Less work for police force
Medi-Cal minus healthcare
Plus HMO equals fast death—
Of course...

I know these parts
I know these parts...

Well!!!

Big City, Bright Lights

Yester-year
Was a year of revelation and reflection
While pacing the block

Overwhelmed with the thought
Of how many clocks stopped
In Inglewood
Los Angeles
Compton
Watts

I used to take it one day at a time
While blowing ganja to Hendrix
Now I take it
One hour at a time
Good brother Dee Black
Told me to count the minutes

'Cause life is short
Death is certain
In the 'hood
Youngsters are prone
To unfriendly fire

So I take it down like a shot
Of 100-proof
Grabbing the AX
Whacking the bush
For not bringing home the troops

Oh, yeah!
They will twist ya
In these

United Snakes of America
Where we eat in the homeless's face
And turn away when they stare atcha!
Mad 'cause they're asking you for spare change
But if you were in their position
You would do the same thang!!!

Speak easy
Knock on wood
'Cause life can change
In the blink of an eye
PLEASE BELIEVE THAT!

Young man
Pull up your pants
Put down the drink
THINK!
Stop asking where the weed at

The Marcus Garvey story
Yep!
You should read that
And discuss with your peeps
To receive feedback...

In this big city
Filled with bright lights
Where we go from freeze tag
To fist fights
To popping artillery at each other
Throughout the night!!!

We Be Watts Fathers

Offspring of Eastside wisdom
Neighborhood watching over our children
We been there
In there
Seldom getting credit
Indebted to big mommas,
Grandpas, pa-pas, pops, dads
Uncles, big homies that showed us the way
Saving the day
By any means necessary
So it's only necessary
That we give thanks for Watts fathers
Offspring of Eastside wisdom
Navigating the village
Shielding our children/
Scrubbing targets off their backs
In treacherous terrain
We remain in our children's lives
With or without wives, we still there!
Baby mama drama, we still there!
Systematic attacks, we still there!
Go to jail, touchdown, we still there!
Welfare tried to replace us, we still there!
We there!
What'chall thot!?
We'll leave?
Run off?
Nope... not in our DNA
'Cause we be Watts fathers
Offspring of Eastside wisdom
Neighborhood watching over our children
Strong, solid, dark, light, chocolate, brown
Nickersons, PJ's, Jordan Downs...
We still here!!!!!

Watts, 1926, '65, '92, uprising ... we still here!
Rising up out of the concrete jungle
Humble, whole, young, old, bold
We stroll with so much soul,
'Cause we be...
Watts fathers ... offspring of Eastside wisdom...
Neighborhood watching over our children....

Ride

Four deep
In a four-door Caprice
No Ls
Reeking of kush smell
Meditating on heaven while dwelling in hell
As I pop-lock upside down
In East Ethiopian Congo Square
Dancing with goons in guerilla garb
Keeps me on my tippies
Up rocking through Sanford
Passing through Ferguson and Oakland
To get back to Watts...
Sankofa vision
Visualize this urban mystic beast
Black turban tilted east
Pouring loose-leaf
Lavender licorice libation
For the young ancestors...

Devin Brown,
Kendrec McDade,
Ezell Ford,
Sean Bell,
Trayvon Martin,
Timothy Stansbury,
Michael Brown,
Oscar Grant,

We say asè

Popping that fire back at them
Having them back up and stop killing our children
So we ride
Like it's no tomorrow
Dipping through 'hoods and boroughs
Sorrows drowned in West Afrakan rum
Run, young black man, run
Make it home
Hug your family
And we gon' roam like cell phones
Brownies and hoodies on
Searching for assassins
Of black and brown
Lower and upperclassmen
Fasting in a Ramada
Kumbaya Obatala Chango chant
Summonsing the spirits of Trayvon Martin and Oscar Grant
Blessings granted in a BART station
Skittle flavored
Make-it-home wishes…
For all my babies targeted to come up missing
Listen…

To all my soldiers
Salute your tribes
Hop inside the whips and let's RIDE!!!

Tribal Chant

Darker tribe
Melanin young Twa
Obatala Yirmiya Oga
Allah
All that
All black
Coming atcha
It's best you fall back!

Aboriginal Watts,
At the minimal, betta watch—
For young riders,
Eastsiders...
Reppin' Watts life
From a project front porch,
Universal, flag,
Truth be the torch

"We are more alike, my friends, than we are unalike."
 – Maya Angelou
Children of the sun,
Daughters of the moon,
Home of the goons,
Connected through the struggle,
Place us anywhere on Earth, we gon' bubble,
And explode, into a cloud of purple haze,
Melanin activation to make it through the maze...
It amazes me,
How creatively,
We weave everything we be—

From a tapestry of Big Momma's croquette,
My name is Oshea,
Markham Junior High,
Wife went to Foshay,
Heard dem say...
We be poetry's Bey & Jay,
Thanks for the props
But you can call us Food & Socks!

We keep it hot like Ozzie & Ruby Dee,
What haters think 'bout dat?
Nothing to do with me,
We don't budge,
We keep it in the blood,
Royal lineage,
That gave birth to the Love

Bruh!

You can catch us in the ethers wit' it,
Blessing the people—
Swinging like a preacher wit' it!

It's been a minute,
Since we had a talk, brother,
You know Food,
But you don't know The Darker Brother,
Reppin' Watts life—
From a project front porch,
Universal flag,
My truth be the torch!

Hard Liquor

- Straight Shots, No Chaser -

"I love you but I don't like you ... so I'm gonna help you so I don't hurt you!"

-Linda Jefferson

Shots Fired

pathetic hater
sorry excuse for blackness
sadness behind a computer screen
screaming at deaf ears
muted cheers
warranted his drastic measures for attention

Attention! Attention!

read all about him...
he proclaims prominence
yet his providence is cowardice
#1 scum of the village
carpetbagger
poverty pimp
the worst of
what the community has to offer
a plagiarizing author
who's allergic to indexes
vexed at the thought of this imbecile
posing as an intellectual
to those who don't know
his intellect reflects flesh without soul
hole in his core
an infinite scab and sore
to all who listen to his verbal diarrhea
his teachers are Wikipedia
wicked media
and corroded glands

he will never get the respect of MAN!
because an evil intent, always betrays itself in the end
and the world will watch his works fade away
like writings in the sand!

Forgiveness

The wick of my heart
Burns spirit wax
For a world of clueless candles

Food and drugs
Same administration
Serving chicken menstruation
With smiles on their faces

I harufu (smell) demonic intentions
MSG would make dirt taste good
Biological burgers
Deactivating divinity
Stimulating
Animalistic tendencies
In line for aspartame
Enjoying death in a Happy Meal—
Because you wanted to have it your way…

Flagrant & Foul

Nishati imbalance
Can't eliminate
Flesh eater
Who continues to make love to corpse
Digesting a mad cow
Washed down with aspartame
Herbs can't find the contaminated parts of you

Stuck between mbinguni and geb
On a tightrope
Made out of your ex-lover's locs
30 thousand feet in the air
Strands began to unravel
Remembering you scandalous
You beg for forgiveness
From scars you left behind
Msaada starts to give
Loud snap echoes through the night
Falling from borrowed time
Wings cemented in your back
There will be no flying tonight

The chi welcomes your plummet
6 feet deep....

Don't Call

don't call me to talk
'bout adolescent bodies outlined in chalk
marksmen marking bullseyes on our suns' backs
parents sat for 2 years in kitchen window
awaiting suns to come back
and still they wait!!!

Don't call me to talk

I'm busy filling cartridges
with hollows dipped in garlic
target practicing with Zimmerman headshots
40 Glock cocked & tilted slightly
to compensate for kick

Don't call me to talk

I'm tired of yo' talking/
social media posting
boasting 'bout justice
on their network
and when it pop off
you're ghost and it's just us!!!

cannons, hoodies & ski masks
turn crooked cops into straight pigs
so don't call me to talk
I'm busy listening to the voices of Oscar Grant, Devin Brown, Latasha Harlins, Troy Davis & Trayvon Martin … young martyrs in the ancestral realm … realmington steel on my hip, extended clip, ready to trip … So don't call me to talk…
only call me if you're ready to ride!!!

A Problem

She speak swords
Darkness blankets her
Friendly smile hides true intentions

Plotter
Peeped her game long ago
Claiming to be secure
In her insecurities

Tell us the truth
Your nose can only grow so long
Before you start to look deformed
Ms. Dream Killa
Killing dreams is what you do best
Have never seen you in a healthy relationship
Yet
You have relationship advice for days…

Ms. Shape Shifter
Reflecting a dragon-snake mix
Spitting fireballs at mirror
'Cause you hate yourself
Self-hatred got you on a kamikaze mission…

Die slow, snake dragon

Die slooooow…

The Scene

Soothsayers....
fellowshipping in speakeasies
with child-support papers tucked neatly in their pockets
spirits stored in attic
sold to whomever seems to care for the moment

She offers façade smirks
nodding in agreement to his babbling on stage
Mr. Conscious walks in...
talking on cell phone in high pitch
arguing with Momma for not cleaning his room
sage burns, forcing shyest tongues to tie
reticence engulfs room
till ancient aroma evaporates

Open-mic veteran fidgets in seat
intentionally walks out
on newbie's piece
returning when name is called...
miraculously appearing
to speak to self
had lost the crowd
before breath
uttering falsetto, baritone, garbage
rushing off stage
leaving like actually having a life to go home to....

Griots, tajedis, storytellers,
keepers of this most sacred word
stop jacking off on stage and releasing on your audience
impregnating their minds with dis-eased semen
leaving them to give birth to retarded situations nine
months later...

Young Hopeful

When I speak trues
I drop jewels
In hopes that you scoop one up and swallow
Allowing hollow inside to illuminate
Projecting light
In turn
Lighting the wick of some young girl's soul
Encouraging her to keep legs closed
Holding on to treasure
Forever if she never finds someone
Worthy of her sacredness
Staple this
Note to her heart
So her chest will twitch
Every time she senses
a young PUNK trying to run game
Princess
Make them
Remember
Your name
BEAUTIFUL

Divinity is your birthright!

We need more rites of passages
For the bastards
Plaguing our tribe
With tainted semen
Passing shortcomings
Hang-ups
Through genetic make-ups
Assuring offspring to be fucked up
Just like them...

I love them
But I don't like them
So I'ma help them
So I don't have to HURT them...

Young ... hopeful.

I've been reserved
Observing this Los Angeles poetry scene from a distance
Distant lovers at best ... that clash when truth spews
Dues aren't paid through mic masturbation
You must do more than jack off on stage...

Young ... hopeful.

Telling us what's wrong with the world is redundant/
We hear it all the time
How 'bout what's wrong with you/
Change self/ those close to you will follow suit!

Crowd tunes out
When poets don't believe their work!
You can see it in their eyes/
Disconnected through one-sided, fanciful stories of triumph!
Can we hear 'bout a time when you got your ass whipped?
Playing with this gift will never manifest magic...
You will grow old & mute on first floor of skyscraper...

Tell us...
Do any of your pieces reference theses of
Teachers that came before you?

Homage should be paid whenever you utter
Words to a listening audience/Who are you?
Where do you come from?
Can anyone vouch for your rhetoric?
Or you just a loose cannon
Aiming aimlessly at your reflection in the mirror?

Who were you before? Tell them...
I command!!!
I already know
Your disposition shouts your past experiences...
You've never loved yourself
But expect others to "Like" you on Facebook!

I will not lie to you!

Stop swimming in waters that you can stand up in!

The deep end awaits your plunge
Without life jacket on...

So jump!

And meet me where sharks prey on weaklings...
I will be there...
FEASTING on sharks!!!
I hope you arrive sooner than I expect...
So I can welcome you...
Give thanks...
And say

Let's eat together!!!

Young Hopeful...

Foggy Mirrors

Forgive me
with the blood of your convictions
till I wear your pain in lifelines
I can't call you to use
I blame myself
for believing I was ever the cause of your UGLY!

The square root of your truth
resides on your tongue
saliva creates lava & alkaline
depending on ... intentions
yield to righteousness
allow words to exit you divine

Ink faults, regrets, blame
fold ignorance of yourself
into paper airplane
then fly it away from your matter...
creating space to receive your pretty
stunning abstract canvases
hanging from the walls of your thot chamber

Frequent your inner exhibit
showcase its wonders to the world
be not frightened
to fall on your face
like a clumsy magician
discovering magic & gravity are not the same thing

Pardon My Tears

At 5 –
I was told she expired herself
tears of a child
taken for granted when—
caption reads...

YOUR GRANDMOTHER KILLED HERSELF!!!

Freedom hid between—
torn pages of family albums
cemented together in a Waco, Texas grave plot—

Stories pass through ovarian cancer
shows 21-gun salute with only one shell casing
deficient answers tainted–
pelt back sores Granny left behind
missed her by few years...
birthed into violence
snooze-walking day imaginings
where wilted trees
breed strange fruit with her face
circuitous brutality
whipped my soul into torn scriptures
where I've spent most of life
Krazy-Gluing an existence
with merely half the story

Memorandum sent
returned, marked
"look within"
plucking the chords of the universe
as a distant star...
broke organ

playin' origins of my genetic make-up
off-beat in A minor / B-flat
probing for answers—
subsequently
it came 40 moons into a Watts equinox
she released herself
so I could learn
the highest act of spirit...

Forgiveness!

Whom It May Concern

Ladies
if you think a good man is hard to find
STOP looking in the trashcan...

Husbands don't hang out in dumpsters
unless they're dumpster diving
to survive a moment of despair
recycling bottles & cans
headed to the thrift store
to upgrade their gear
button-down
wool blazer
thick piece of leather
holding up trousers
that's a man right there!

Can change your oil,
replace brakes,
renovate your home,
and bake,
a red velvet cake,
upside down—
sideways ... like it's nobody's business,
have you walking bowlegged,
pigeon-toed,
knock-kneed,
backwards to the water cooler at work,
dosing off smiling ☺ ...about last night...
like it's nobody's business!

Good sista,
he's searching for you!
Just blinded by your dog-filled trashcan,
He can't see you!

"Knowing that I am finally enough, is like discovering dessert is delicious following a disastrous meal."

-Wanda Coleman

Desserts

-Bitter, Sweet, Tasty, Complete-

"Truth comes to us from the past, then, like gold washed down from the mountains."

-Carter G. Woodson

The Fireplace

The crackling of the Wood's history—
reads lopsided on a Broadside,
ancestors kept their eyes wide
not to get broadsided,
searching for fair views on Fairview—
yet, views were only fair
from a rocking chair of privilege.

Summer of '22
37 neighbors wore hoods in neighborhoods—
terrorizing black lives before the matter.
Ku Klux Klan 'n'em
banned from the city of
soon-to-be champions in '31—
for serving 31 flavors of vanilla injustices—
pressing chocolate into cones
 that burst indigo rage in '65.
29 negroes of 63,000 residents—
read 60's census report,
melanin flipped fraction—
upside right—
by the time
showtime landed at the Forum in '73...
...releasing purple & gold rays of magic
into a Hollywood Track
that raced thoroughbreds when
American dollars were backed by gold.

Old racist covenants—
exploded into a backdrop of Edward Vincent—
causing whites to flee by '83—
leaving black & brown tension—
brewing thick gravy like
into a stew that was separated but equal

healing and lethal
deprived and regal
like Paul piercing poverty with prosperity needles...

This Ingle
where Tyra banks at Broadway Federal
to keep resources with the people

This Ingle
fireplace
historic chimney
burning hope in a South Bay stem of opportunity
igniting unity via an unspoken language of
young Deandre offering to carry Guadalupe's bags through
the woods; lil Cesar helping Ms. Addie cross the street at
Manchester and Nutwood.

This Ingle
fireplace
historic chimney
where poets, artists, and elders
congregate on a Thursday night
to vibrate ether like
in a holy cipher
word orchestra, literary choir
blessing the city with prayer offerings
from a wood stage covered in oral libation
giving thanks for having the liberty to
explore our artistic vocation...

This Ingle
fireplace
historic chimney
that will one day
be the last great gasp for solidarity...

Destiny's Certainty

George's long neck
Permits him to look out for his tribe,
Bible to his side,
Knowing the battle that's approaching
will not be physical
Lump in his throat,
As he observes
a different type of storm fast approaching,
Kisses his wife Natalie, gently as morning dew
Suddenly, levees blew up
Catastrophic flood,
George transitioned,
Natalie survived,
And relocated to Los Angeles to live in streets,
Pushing a basket filled with her life,
Her face glows
as she remembers George's last kiss—

Frown on another woman's face—
While leaving church—
In a brand-new Mercedes—
'Cause Sister Smith didn't speak to her,
And pastor didn't remember her name
The two ladies meet in the intersection
of King & Avalon,
Church lady distracted by yelling at her son—
For falling asleep earlier at service
BAM!!!!!!!!!!
Car strikes Natalie,
She and belongings fly through air—
Landing in George's arms.
They're together again…

Katrina will not be able to reach them now…

Prepare for Takeoff!

Ask elders for permission
before you open yours.
Rites of passage—
passing through—
cocoon to caterpillar.

Wings begin to sprout,
flying is inevitable,
do not jump the process.

 Heart races,
 you're close to the edge.

Congo sound your pulse...
time to jump.
Everyone's watching...

3, 2, 1...

Wake Up

People of the world ... please, wake up!!!!

Make up lost time with our children
It's time to love each other
Hug each other
The world will not get better
If we only hurt each other,
Love mother, father, brother, sister, family...
Forgiving those who wrong us!!!
Creating a beautiful tapestry...

Everybody ... let's wake up!!!

Make up lost time with our children
Hand balls can turn into hand guns ...
Causing random
Acts of violence
Against grandsons and goddaughters
If we don't teach love
Peace and soul in our households

Wake up, teachers...

Listen to our children
They are bored, brilliant geniuses...
Who deserve to be heard...
So we can teach in the languages of their hearts

Giving them a funny word in passing
Laughing cures brokenness
And gives birth to humanity...

Wake up, students...
You are the future....
Do you know what that means?

You can be anything!!!
Lawyers, doctors,
Business owners,
Kings and queens

Heaven sent...
It's evident...   you can be anything!!!

Even the

United States of America's president!!!

Independence

Torn
date my
daughter was born
fireworks
for a country
built on
backs of slaves
I
condemn
the latter
and celebrate
Princess Shai

Thinking

Organized our practices
served them back to us
like they're new

Much pepper on artificial messages
releasing unrelieved info through nostrils

Aaaaa-chooo

Preschool
teased
because my hair knotted up
like black fist in the 60s
everyone want to rock locs now...
society says it's cool
cooling under shaded trees
think how many of my ancestors were hung
whipped and chained under shaded tree...
and how our seeds
cop whips and chains
without remembering the lashes
under a shaded tree...
don't mind me...
I'm just thinking

Soul Mate

Met her five eons ago
Still smell her in my dreams
Gerbera daisy scent
Black waters
Purple skies
Rosary beads
Fancy the arc of her perfection
Blue lotus
Spirit child
Jive talking in tongues
Kneeling
Praying
Dancing
In gold arrogance
Scrubbing targets
Off the backs of our offspring...

Questions

Twenty-five moons ago
I began to ask questions
No answer
Just shhhh . . .
So I started listening
Everyone wanted to follow him
After scrutinizing his message
He says
Follow yourself
The kingdom is inside of you
Translating papyrus
To pastors
Met with eyebrow raised
Torrent eyes
Wrinkled forehead

Where's this child getting this from?

Tapping my chest
Twenty-five moons later
They're asking me for clarity

And I reply . . . "It's in you."

Myths

Muted lips
There's no J
In Hebrew language
Pounding information into brick heads
Doesn't work like holidays
Westernized scroll
Twisted
Two months added
Old deception stories
Aren't muted anymore

First Immaculate Conception
On walls of pyramid

Heru ... is the name

Rain Forest

Daydream into Tanzanian terrains
Channeling rain in time of drought
Village can thrive again
Children can bathe again

Awake and carved wood blocks
Into tribal face to remember journey

Soldiers
Time travel
When chewing
Baby umbrellas
Insist
I partake
Graciously
I decline

Standing in absolute
No need to ask again
Tap into me and travel
Again and again

Giving thanks for the never-ending journey

Dark Matter

Spirits
Having human experiences...
I am you

You are me

Time traveler
With compass
Atop crown chakra

I am nothing
Formless matter
That matters to everything

Son, brother, father, nephew, cousin, friend
Enemy, king, prince, peasant, god

I am everyone that's wronged you...
I am everyone that's done you right...
I am nothing
So I am everything

I'm ever changing...

Youthful Steps

Binoculars
On my third eye
Allow me to see through folks
Transparent, hollow bodies
Walking zombies
My beard soaked

Tears of warrior passion
Uncontrollable compassion

We are better than this
They say it's in the genes . . .
Whatever Moms and Pops do—
You do…

The pavement is watching our steps

Cement tells stories
If only we listen more
Talk less

Give youth
Different path to choose
To stop feeling lost
Before they lose

M.J.

Half-century of
Whirlwind spin
Dropped jaws
Moon Walked
Before Neil Armstrong

Transformed into legend
Remained child at heart
Rooted in Mother's soil
Grew into man with feeble branches
That the world hung on to...

Breaking was inevitable
Healing through sound
Sing, Mike, sing
Dance, Mike, dance
Soar, Mike, soar

We see you...

Whole

There she is
Matriarch's daughter
Generation of strong black women
Right eye fierce
Left strong
Knows future
Between legs
Nature's essence
Balanced ovaries

There he is
Zulu shaman
Medicine man
Healing worlds
Untainted semen
They spend dynasties together
Transcend Earth
Wrap Orion's belt 'round waist
Pulling galaxies jointly
Aliens chant names
For goodness' sake
Love into
Sand castles
Coated in steel
Standing
Still
In the midst of chaos

There they are…
There they are…

WHOLE!!!

Mind's Eye

My inner-eye wears locs
to see all from a street perspective
Mystical, esoteric, perception beyond ordinary
Receiving spiraling will of crystallized energy
Instruments playing under water,
engaging whales to waltz
Signaling sharks to blow kisses at goldfish
In unison with embryos backstroking in uma, womb
Birthing a new nation of thots
Manifesting destinies
through muted, indigenous languages
Aligning matter into liquid
Forming avatars,
charged with not handing over our legacy... Again!
All seeing vibratory senses
Nyeusi mind
Nyeusi thots
Roho singing our hymns
in Big Momma's shower voice
Pa-Pa's profanity wrapped in...
bet-back for a thousand, SUCKA!!!
Vanity distorted my cerebral cortex
Remembering things I really want to forget
Cerebellum needs tune-up
When retinas project bootleg images
of what I think I see
Equilibrium
Balanced on Mom's fallopian tubes
Orbiting Ra's stare as an orphan
Receiving vitamin D from sun
To decode encrypted messages...
Written in galaxy scribble on Watts project brick

No Defeat

Murmuring skeletons of surrender
Waving flags of truce
Battered poets
Stoned by scholars
Intellectual analysis
Knifing through moyo
Leaving tongues tied
Belching like dirty carburetor
Milk-carton sorry expressions—
Circulate to young hopefuls
Reminding them how not to look defeated
Hold worries between knuckles
Uppercut doubts from your attention
Write divinity you dreamt about...
Faint standing up
Until luja is all we kusikia

POETS!!! Hypnotize your listeners
Helicopter-shred their previous thoughts–
Till their souls smile at your spirit

Canvas your words
On walls of venues
For when you're absent
They'll scream in your defense
Scatter stanzas across
Heart chakras
Chant beneath wings of sightless eagles
WRITERS & POETS
In your rest
Make us...
Search the skies for your poetry

An Olmec's Sankofa

She flew into her future
backwards...
fertilizing crops from teardrops –
coated in memories of where she's come from
simultaneously accessing both realms

Cosmos/pyramids
Amenta/rain forest
ethers/Watts

Observing him
through ozone layer...
thick-lipped
strong-faced
Afrakan sculpture of antiquity
sculpting a masterpiece for always –
mirroring reflection

As she flies by...
he bows
knowing –
his existence is in her wings
she smiles...

Assuring –
his story will be told
he rejoices
legacy's protected
etched in a stoned memory

Casualties

In third-world countries
malady comes in 31 flavors
without the cold stones.
War seen thru one million eyes at once
casting various vantage points
blurring the truth.

Yet out of these perfectly wounded worlds
elimu hovers the nocturnal rustling of optimism,
so thick that it latches to the core of souls
that recognize its majesty
stepping over corpses
remembering atrocities
of the innocent
I am here
a survivor
seeking approval from ancestors
legacies embedded
in the holograms of their absence
charged with not letting their missions become
only wingless dreams
burned in their skulls
this will not be their legacy
when my pen
is dipped
in
their DNA.

Asè

-Tributes, Honors, Reflections-

Give Thanks...

For Richard Dedeaux

From New Orleans to Watts,
We watched
Gumbo and barbeque
Mixed into a cool, smooth,
Unapologetic Watts legend

 Man without measure
Los Angeles treasure
Louisiana, New Orleans hot peppa!!!
Dashed over Jordan Jr. High School in the 1950s...
Brewing in an Eastside...
Watts Writers' Workshop Crock-Pot in the 1960s,
Where he mixed verbs, adjectives, and soliloquies
Into a tapestry of creativity...

Angry Voices on the Streets in Watts
A Rising Sun /

Heru - Hero / we're so / blessed to have known...

Baba Dedeaux !!!

1970s had them *Rappin' Black in a White World*
Richard's a cold piece of black-arts history
Power to the people / people powered /
Standing the test of antiquity
Louisiana bayou boy,
Mud Town, Jordan Downs teen
Haitian revolution pulsates in his genes

God's DNA
Divine fingerprints
Printing sacred scrolls

New Orleans voodoo
Congo square
Makin' magic
Between "gy" and "rate"
Drum circle of chest
Yirmiyah, Obatala, Chango quest thru triple light
Here and there at once
Richard Dedeaux is out of sight

Griot
Tejadi
Scribe of this most sacred word
Speaking truth to power from the curbs to the suburbs

And "when the 90s came"
Richard did not miss a beat...
Voice for the voiceless...
Ambassador for the streets...

Heru - Hero / we're so / blessed to have known...

Baba Dedeaux !!!

Dee Black

Dee Black / D-Negro / D-Neyusi

Triple light reflects
Gnostic gangsta's brim tilted east
Cutty mac revolutionary
Revolutionizing Leimert
One good brother at a time!
Fellowshipping with inhabitants
Under mud-cloth covered sky...

Top of da morning
Via spiritual text blast
Teacher of immortality

Dee Black / D-Negro / D-Neyusi

One finger in the air
For the cuttys that ain't here
His mantra
Nag Hammadi decoder
Ancient mysticism in his disposition
Sprinkling spirit parables on the eardrums of lost souls
Children of concrete
Squatting Afrakan style
Giving thanks & praises
Receiving nuggets of wisdom
From this regal warrior for righteousness

Dee Black / D-Negro / D-Neyusi

Long-shoe shaman
Mayor of Leimert

Majestic enveloped notes
Sealed in antiquity
To be opened in the eye of the troubled
No worries...
Pop's on point
Father to the fatherless
Shadowboxing with boogeyman so Bubba don't have to fight!!!

Dee Black / D-Negro / D-Neyusi

Slow dancing in eternity's gaze with his princess Quran
Atop Dogon constellation—
In preparation for the birth of a god / goddess
Modest when being exalted
Exalting others was effortless for him
Hymns of sacred sopranos
Lead him to his loved ones on the other side
Yaya / Baba await his galactic arrival!
Maat releases king to triple light
Mathu and Gay reverence in the moment
As the village cheers
Drums drum
Dancers dance

For...

Dee Black / D-Negro / D-Neyusi

For Jessica Cleaves

Have you ever heard the sun sing
Through the voice of a princess in a dreamy, majestic alto
Redefining range and ballads
With vocal wizardry in a piercing falsetto
Weaving heartstrings with an agave-nectar soaring voice?

Eyes of a dreamer
Dreaming eyes
Radiating through a young woman disguised
As a lullaby, lullaby by our angelic earth angel
But all good-byes, don't mean gone...

Queen Jessica Cleaves lives on and on through songs
And memories...
Remembering how she really, really envied the sunshine
The irony is she's now shining with the sun
Singing with the sun
Earth, wind, and fire
Wrapped in friends of distinction
She's now grazin' in the grass of the heavens
Of the heavens, of the heaven...
Baby, can you dig that?!!!

I really hope you do ... shine, Jessica, shine...
You know we would rather have you ... though whenever
The sun shines, we got you!!! Shining through!!!
The world will miss you!!!
But as you say ... we can send a gram/ send a gram
Telegram from Earth to the heavens

To get in touch with you
Any way we can ... by letter or by hand
We can funk with you
Hear from you ... when we read the small print!!!

Sooooo ... have you ever heard the sun sing
Through the voice of a queen in a dreamy, majestic alto
Redefining range and ballads
With vocal wizardry in a piercing soprano?
Yes, we all have...
Through the incomparable,
Immeasurable, falsetto-alto-soprano
Of Queen Jessica Cleaves

Tribute to a King

Watts
By way of
Compton and New Orleans
Viral and abroad
Mystical maverick
Black spiritual magic pulsates his genes
This is a tribute to a King

King Richard
A doctor's doctor
Scholar's scholar
Father's father
Scribing with Tehuti Thoth
Carving molds of brilliance on sacred scrolls
Resilience of Pharaohs
Dynasty shaped from his pineal aptitude
The magnitude of his work is beyond sight
Challenging us to develop insight to see beyond sight
Insightfulness
In sight, fullness is actualizing
To see what our eyes can't realize
Real eyes reside in third-eye apparition
Visions of gods thru human conditions
Dark matter
Dr. King showed us why darkness matters
Through the power of melanin in the brain
Vitamin D passes through blood stream
As sunlight penetrates skin
Melatonin released when sun goes down
Neophyte virtues birth inner vision
Into suns of light...
Activating your pineal gland
Allowing you to see at night!

Sound eye, I of Heru, Ra
Consciously aware to move thru your Ka
Spirit
Don't fear it
Protect it
Projecting your mind to transcend space and time...
Becoming a telepathic super-mental computer
Accessing files of any ancestor's memory
That makes up your bloodline
Great, great, multiplied by 100s
Of great-great grandparents' minds...
Equals the ability to tap into past, present, and future times
A living god on Earth,
In the physical,
Melanin: A Key to Freedom
"The Black Doorway to Amenta"
Check Dr. King's diaries,
African Origin of Biological Psychiatry

A psychiatrist for lost souls
Referencing lost scrolls
Ben-Ben stone
Black Dot,
Shabaka Stone,
Aquarian Spiritual Center
Center of Black Gnostic Studies
Scrutinizing Kush, Kemet
With the vision of Dogons
Rising from prince to king
Under the tutelage of Alfred and Bernice Ligon
Aquarians in the bookstore...
Storing books in his unlimited brain capacity
Baba King
Father King
Namaste for sharing your dream
Cuz this right here is a tribute to a King
The melanin man, resting at the Temple of Millions of Years
The final journey of the soul to God's land...

Baba Baraka

Almighty
Literary giant
Stirring prose
Into black magic
Blessed prince,
Shuffling a deck of cards
With faces of Coltrane, Monk
Malcolm and Sun Ra

Baraka dealt the *Hard Facts*
To a people declaring, *"It's Nation Time!"*
Founder of the Black Arts Movement
Which transcended time
Space, worlds of limitation...
He embodied *The Essence of Reparations*
When the folds of history
Reference the greats
He's in that conversation...

His words are bottled like rich scotch
Fermented in our brains
Poured in times of libation
Baba, we will always remember your name...
Works
Hurts
Love
Sentiments—
For the human experience...
That enriched lives...
Gave writers of the world—
A solid vantage of what mastery—
Looks like
Feels like
Heals like...

We are now healed
Whole and complete
From hearing you speak...
Reading your literature
Scriptures
The *Preface to a Twenty Volume Suicide Note*
"Must be the devil, must be the devil"
"Dope"
Funk Lore
"Somebody Blew Up America"
The truth in your work
Had this country in hysteria!
Master of writing drama
Non-fiction, fiction, activist, and poet extraordinaire
Acclaimed editor, playwright, essayist
Over 35 plays and 50 books
His work is everywhere...

Distinctive slacks, button-down—
Gleaming leather grown-man shoes
Wool blazer, fine scarf, bebop and signature frames—
That said, "I see you."

Oh, Baba Baraka, rest well in paradise...
We see you, too ... blessed prince.

Thank you for shining your light!

Breast Cancer (Breast Can Serve)

Woman
most startling being in world
way she birth universe
pull studio apartment out purse
always have extra Bible verse
to share for healing...
willing to go extra mile
to see you smile...

Oh, magnificent woman ... we see you/ honor you

She is beautifully nestled in a
sea of healing
she walk upright and speak with love
her smile is beyond marvelous
as we bask in her overflow
praise fills her heart
worship has been her priority
she handles the word of God like ninth-century crystal
intensely listening through meditation
one day, she feels lump in her chest
no stress ... with God, all things are possible

It's breast cancer// breast can serve
as a reminder of how mighty God is
still...
they say she must
cut her hair for chemo
we know...
she be beautiful
with or without hair...
we stare in amazement
at how wonderfully

created she is...
she is...
Big Momma prayers over
Mississippi suppertime

Oh, magnificent woman...
you are the reason
worlds turn
girls learn to discern
before they can talk
crawl before they walk
into purpose, greatness,
destiny, destined to be
a reflection of she, her, lady...

Oh, magnificent woman...

Do you hear birds humming?
it's because angels are summoned
to protect you
daughter of Big Momma
mother of three
this diagnosis can't stop your glee...
praise, smile, laughter, worship,
because breast cancer is limited
and woman, you are
an infinite field of unfolding possibilities
sewn together in Granny's crocheted
pink ribbon
to remember how far you come
to share your testimony
breast cancer/ breast cancer
breast can serve as a reminder
Of how mighty God is...

For Bee

I remember Watts summers
Pomegranate & loquat trees
Water-hydrant showers
Throw'em up tackle in the middle of the street...
Nanas, papas
Mothers, fathers,
Brothers, sisters,
Homeboys, homegirls...

But Bee...

I will always remember her ... as woman!!!

Graceful, keen, resilient,
Gatherer of honey
From the flowers of life...
Pollinating her family's bouquet
The stem of baby's breath over loving siblings
Sisters represented by daisies, sunflowers & roses
Accented by the strong branches of her three brothers...

Nurtured and watered by Queen Mother ... Ms. Grays...

You see,
I remember Buck-a-Bag Man,
Doughnut trucks,
Spending nights at the big house
Playing Atari and left-hand give it up...

House cleaner than Clorox...
Refrigerator full of food...
Doors always were open

When me and WeDog came to visit dude...

But Bee...
I will always remember her ... as woman!!!!

Strong, honest,
Beautiful, distinct voice...
Looking through mess
Bringing out others' greatness...

Encouraged, complimented, and smiled at little ole me...
Seeing prominence in me,
When I did not see it in myself...

You see,
I remember a lot of things in my life...

But Bee...

I will always remember her ... as woman!!!

Latasha Harlins

Fifteen years old
Dreams
Goals
In her head
Westchester High School student
Sparked uprising
Here we go again; here we go again
Juice and gin was our choice of beverage back then
On block of Watts, screaming, "F'k the cops!"
Rodney wasn't a shock!
Just happened to get caught on tape
But Latasha getting shot
By Korean store owner had us HOT!
It didn't make sense
Two times
Korean lady pleads self-defense
Huh?
Judge Karlin
Reduced sixteen-year sentence
Five years probation
Four hundred hours of community service
Doing our community a major disservice

IT'S TIME TO RIDE!!!

"We gotta redefine the public-safety narrative in this country; otherwise, we will keep getting 'more police' as a response, when we need healing, wellness, and recovery services."

-Aqeela Sherrills

Borrowed Angel (Devin)

Mother's comfort
helps in Earth's layover
way over yonder
he grew from baby
to young man
on a Compton front porch
where storks don't deliver babies
black mothers do...
...and every black brother—

DON'T DO DIRT!

This hurt
searching for meaning through
skateboards, basketball, and photography
this gotta be a wake-up call, y'all
to stop the killings in our neighborhoods
good neighbors are moving out
leaving us with just 'hoods...

Devin's good
producing beats in God's orchestra
skateboarding on clouds
kick flip
Ollie
Indy
ride, Devin, ride...
crossing over angels
back spin
through the legs
no-look pass
jumping from the free-throw line
fly, Devin, fly

Devin did not die
he transitioned
a musician with the best gig
a baller on the greatest team
God's photographer
capturing our dreams....

So dream high
make all goals lateral
battle is inevitable
we just can't put our souls up for collateral

Let's remember Devin
as a borrowed angel that Mother comforted
on Earth's layover
way over yonder
where he grew from baby
to young man
on a Compton front porch
where storks don't deliver babies
black mothers do...
...and every black brother—

DON'T DO DIRT!

That Dude (Stephan A. Grays)

The baby of the matriarch's nest
That marched his 1st into 1974
As a Pisces, sun, brother, cousin, friend
Four sisters
Two brothers
He was the seventh of them...
112th and Mona Ave.
Manifested 112 ways for me, WeDog and Tommy to say...
We love you from a Watts backyard walnut tree...
Stephan
Stepping his magic into our lives as toddlers
Knee-high to grasshoppers
We went back like Atari and ColecoVision
Me saying, "Ask Ms. Grays if we can spend the night."
So we can be up late night
Watching the Playboy Channel
But acting like were playing Intellivision...

That Dude!

The first cat I ever climbed a tree with
Found girls to play Hide and Go Get It with
Sat at the Grays' beautiful dining room table
And had Thanksgiving dinner with...

That Dude!

That smelled everything
From his hands to a cup of water or a plate of food...
If you got too close...
He'd smell you too!

This means he was always present and tapping into his senses...
A private man with the gift of discernment—
That tried to choose wisely who he let hop over his fences...

That Dude!

A baby lover
True Baba
Quick to get on the floor wit'cho Bèbè kids
And go into his goo-goo-ga-ga

That Dude!

So sharp, shrewd,
Walked smooth
Talked even smoother
Cooler than the other side of the mattress
No phony façades or tactics
If he had it
You had it
If he didn't
He'd go get it...
So strong in his survival steelo
With passion that would rival any 21st century CEO...

Many cats have come before him
Many more will come after and act so smooth

But as for me and my tribe
Stephan A. Grays
Will always be the one and only...

That Dude!!!

Champagne

"We don't just borrow words; on occasion, English has pursued other languages down alleyways to beat them unconscious and rifle their pockets for new vocabulary."

-Booker T. Washington

A Toast to Spoken Word

-My Poetry Thread-

As a student of words, I've always been fascinated with their texture and sway, particularly how when a word is expressed in a different tone, it can convey many contrasts of the same shade. The vibration of language interosculates words together and shapes communication that culturally grounds a people into its fertile soil.

There are many biblical accounts of creation that have begun with the word, and from the word these accounts support the idea that everything in the Universe has come into being through the spoken word. People can explore this verity by simply examining their lives up until this point, and evaluating their use of words, language, and intent to see if their lives are in exact proportion to the words they have chosen to speak. Scientific studies have also shown us that words carry vibrations, and these vibrations release frequencies that can be measured for intensity and intent. I suppose this is because in order to speak a word, you must have sound, breath, and meaning, which ignites this phenomenon called the spoken word.

The use of language through the spoken word dates back to the beginning of existence itself. Words represent instruments of speech that are used to transmit one's sentiments to another entity or being. Likewise, one can praise, curse, summon, or dismiss by exercising the employment of the spoken word.

In Afrakan culture, the griot, who is the village's storyteller and historian, is responsible for passing down events, stories, and legacies via the spoken word. Griots are revered in this oral tradition, and are relied upon to educate the masses on their tribal history, religion, and also give the village a sense of purpose and identity.

Many of our ancestors who came to America in chains from Afraka during the widely documented slave trade brought with them sacred rituals from their Afrakan traditions that were practiced and clandestinely shared with the slave communities of the South. Although it was illegal for slaves to read and write at this time in America, many were able to memorize in great detail the rituals, songs, and poetry from our great Afrakan past.

The griot's immeasurable practice survived the slave ships and plantations despite the white slave owners' desecration of the Afrakan culture. There were many enslaved poets and wordsmiths at this time whose names have vanished due to their dignified and admirable gifts. In the mid 16th century, American society only kept records and archived those black poets and writers who were considered patriots of its white agenda. Furthermore, through these accounts we now know that in 1773, a Senegalese enslaved woman name Phillis Wheatley became the first black American poet to publish a book of poems. The book, *Poems on Various Subjects, Religious and Moral,* brought Ms. Wheatley to national prominence, and she was also heralded for being the first black American poet to make a living from her writings. It is also of great importance to note that Jupiter Hammon, a black American writer who was born into slavery, is recognized for being the first black American writer to publish a poem. His poem, "An Evening Thought," first appeared as a broadside in 1761. Mr. Hammon differs from Ms. Wheatley in regards to first-published poem and first-published manuscript. This is not to weaken Mr. Hammon's feat; rather, it is to bring clarity to some of the misrepresented information that has not clearly defined both their roles in black American literature.

By the mid 19th century, abolitionism was at its pinnacle, and leading the poetry brigade was black writer/poet and activist Frances E. Harper, who published her first volume of work, entitled *Poems on Miscellaneous Subjects,* in 1854. Several prominent scholars have contended that Frances's work ushered in the era of black American protest poetry. Frances is also regarded as the first black American to have a short story published in 1861; it was called "Two Offers." This was a significant time in black American poetry, as the reconstruction era (1865-1877) was designed to bring "freedmen" into the society to work and vote as citizens after the Civil War.

In 1893, a young, prolific writer and poet, Paul Laurence Dunbar, published his first volume of poetry, *Oak and Ivy,* and was later celebrated as one of the first Afrakan-American writers to establish a national reputation. Dunbar was also well versed, educated, and a playwright, poet, novelist, and lyricist who occasionally wrote in "negro dialect," associated with the Antebellum South, which fueled much of his early success as a writer and poet. Dunbar's influence on black American poetry would steamroll into the 20th century, as a new generation of poets and artists would later convene in Harlem, New York.

One of these soon-to-be legends who had been influenced by Dunbar was the historian, educator, children's book author, and poet extraordinaire, Arna Bontemps. Born in Alexandria, Louisiana, in 1902, he relocated with his parents to Watts, California, at age three to escape the overtly racial restrictions in the South. Watts had just become a city in 1906, and was rumored to be a great place to raise a family. Watts was certainly a sizzling, vibrant community at this time, and Bontemps would grow up and discover his love for poetry in this atmosphere. Arna Bontemps would later move to Harlem to join one of the first major black poetry movements in America, the Harlem Renaissance, which spanned from the end of World War I through the Great Depression of the 1930s. It is extremely noteworthy that during this time, a shift from individual victories in black American literature to group and collective progression was shaping through poetry.

The Harlem Renaissance originated out of the great migrations of blacks to the North, Midwest, and West Coast in search of better opportunities after World War I. This cultural, social, literary, and artistic explosion drew black writers, artists, musicians, photographers, and poets from all over the world. After moving to Harlem, Arna Bontemps became very good friends with Langston Hughes, who was one of the first Afrakan-American writers to support himself through his writings.

Concurrently, the Black Nationalist movement was thriving in Harlem, New York, as well, led by the seminal political leader, publisher, and Jamaican-born poet Marcus Mosiah Garvey, who on all accounts had spearheaded the UNIA (Universal Negro Improvement Association) into one of the most prolific Black Nationalist movements in the history of the United States of America. At its peak in 1920, the UNIA reported having over four million members. During the next couple of years, Garvey's movement was able to magnetize a gargantuan amount of followers, due in large part from the Cultural Revolution of the Harlem Renaissance and the West Indies immigrants arriving. Garvey's slogan: "One

Aim, One God, One Destiny," was appealing to black veterans settling in Harlem after World War I. Marcus Garvey's movement was also the channel for Malcolm X's mother, Louise, and father, Earl Little to meet at a UNIA convention in Montreal. Earl was the president of the UNIA division in Omaha, Nebraska, and sold the *Negro World* newspaper, for which Louise covered UNIA activities.

During the next forty years (1925-1965), America tightened its grip on blacks across the country. In turn, revolts erupted, cities went up in flames, and a young Malcolm went from street hustler Detroit Red to inmate #22843 to the Nation of Islam's key spokesman, then morphing into the beloved prophet El-Hajj Malik El-Shabazz. When Minister Malcolm was assassinated on February 21st, 1965, coupled with centuries of oppression through global white supremacy, black art and protest poetry would soar to new heights, as the country braced itself for what was to be candid sentiments intended to hold the power structure accountable.

West Coast Poetry Thread

The assassination of Malcolm X grew what I like to identify as my present-day poetry thread. Out of this horrific tragedy, rebellions erupted all over the country; and from this black alliances and writing workshops began to form. The Black Panther Party and US Organization were both shaped from this monumental bang that was heard all around the world.

The Watts Revolt popped off on August 11th, 1965, and shortly after the smoke cleared, Budd Schulberg, an Academy Award-winning screenwriter, came to Watts and started what one attendee said was "the single best writing success story in American history," the 1965 Watts Writers' Workshop. This creative-writing workshop birthed such writers as Raspoet Ojenke, Jayne Cortez, Harry Dolan, Jimi Sherman, Odie Hawkins, Wanda Coleman, The Watts Prophets (Father Amde, Richard Dedeaux, Dee Dee McNeil, and Otis O'Solomon), Johnie Scott, Eric Priestly, the word musician Kamau Daaood, Emory Evans, Curtis Lyle and Quincy Troupe, to name some of the greats.

The Watts Writers' Workshop was generating national buzz and major funding during this time, so much so that the FBI planted informants in the workshop in order to monitor the group's activities. One of these informants, Darthard Perry (aka Ed Riggs), later confessed to burning down the building that housed the workshop, after the group had welcomed him into the sessions with open arms. Although the Watts Writers' Workshop physically lasted for under a decade, members of this acclaimed collective went on to produce film, television, albums, plays, manuscripts, and a large host of other intellectual properties that revolutionized writing, poetry, and protest through the arts.

In 1989, twenty-four years after the Watts Writers' Workshop, this West Coast thread continued to weave as poet Kamau Daaood and master drummer Billy Higgins co-founded The World Stage Performance Gallery in Leimert Park, Los Angeles.

The World Stage offered a drumming and a writing workshop, The Anansi Writers' Workshop. The World Stage has initiated the professions of many great writers as well: Ruth Forman, D Knowledge, V. Kali, Pam Ward, Dee Black, Michael Datcher, Jaha Zainabu, El Rivera, and Conney Williams, to name some. The Anansi Writers' Workshop has been going strong for over 25 years and counting. It has been said to be the child of the Watts Writers' Workshop. This is a direct testament to the gravity and influence of Minister Malcolm's transition and the country's temperature at the time.

East Coast Poetry Thread

Poet and activist LeRoi Jones, largely known as the literary icon Amiri Baraka, would move to New York shortly after Malcolm's death and start the Black Arts Repertory Theater (BARTS), which gave birth to the Black Arts Movement.
TIME magazine described the Black Arts Movement as the "single most controversial movement in the history of African American literature—possibly in American literature as a whole." From this Eastern thread came the likes of poets such as Maya Angelou, Sonia Sanchez, Marvin X, Lucille Clifton, Askia M. Tourè, Etheridge Night, Gwendolyn Brooks, Keorapetse "Willie" Kgositsile, and Nikki Giovanni. The Black Arts Movement was also known as the artistic branch of the Black Power Movement. Many of the writers and poets from this thread would go on to produce a massive amount of acclaimed, incomparable literary works.

In 1968, three years after BAM was taking the literary world by storm, The Harlem Writing Workshop, East Wind, would give birth to the legendary poetry group called The Last Poets, on May 19th, 1968 (the anniversary of Malcolm X's birthday), in Mount Morris Park in Harlem, New York. The Last Poets quickly spiraled from three poets and a drummer to seven young black and Hispanic artists: Gylan Kain, Jalal Nuriddin, Suliaman El-Hadi, Umar Bin Hassan, Abiodun Oyewole, David Nelson, and Felipe Luciano. Out of this assemblage came over 17 albums and countless masterpieces in other formats.

In 1969, this East-Coast quilt continued to expand when poet Gil Scott-Heron heard The Last Poets perform at his school, Lincoln University, in Pennsylvania. After that performance, Abiodun of The Last Poets said Gil Scott-Heron asked him, "Listen, can I start a group like you guys?" From 1970-2011, Gil Scott-Heron went on to record over 25 albums and is heralded as the Godfather of Rap by nearly all that know his legend.

Sewing the Threads Together

One of the biggest bangs that came forth out of these strands that wove into the present day of the hip-hop and rap culture was The Watts Prophets of the West Coast, and The Last Poets and Gil Scott-Heron of the East Coast. This poetry crochet is broadly distinguished as the pioneers of rap, for their hard-hitting, fiery, rhythmic poetry styles that reflected the early stages of what rap would become. This is where the fiber began to weave into the fabric of my generation.

Rolling Stone magazine named The Watts Prophets' 1969 album *The Black Voices: On the Streets in Watts* one of the 40 most groundbreaking albums of all time: "A path-finding moment in the pre-history of hip-hop ... full of minimalist beats and brilliant wordplay nearly a decade before the first recorded rap song."

The 70s would begin with four mammoth, pre-hip-hop albums that gave birth to what rap would eventually avalanche into. Poet Gil Scott-Heron's 1970 debut album release *Small Talk at 125th and Lenox* featured the opening track "The Revolution Will Not Be Televised." This track was able to run through the veins of every inner-city ghetto in the country, tapping into the souls of the people.

One year later, The Watts Prophets' 1971 album release *Rappin' Black in a White World*, and The Last Poets' 1971 album release *This Is Madness* hit the world by blizzard, shaping into the epitome of what it meant to speak truth to power through spoken word.

This brewing volcano further erupted in 1973, with Jalal Nuriddin, aka "Lightnin' Rod," of The Last Poets, and his debut album release *Hustler's Convention*. On this epic, masterful album, Jalal took rhyming to another level and was later credited with being the "Grandfather of Rap."

This is where spoken word, music, and poetry began to interosculate, cultivating into a colossal tree that has weaved branches to every corner of the globe. These branches would later influence soon-to-be hip-hop and rap icons of the 70s, 80s, 90s, and ultimately the new millennium of today.

There is no way to list the infinite number of artists that were influenced directly by The Watts Prophets and The Last Poets and Gil Scott-Heron; however, I'm sure that listing a few will be of great value to many artists that are not familiar with this iconic thread.

Eazy-E, Dr. Dre, DJ Quik, Ice Cube, Ice-T, Tupac Shakur, the L.A. Dream Team, Suga Free, Lupe Fiasco, and O.F.T.B. (Operation From The Bottom) all give the Watts Prophets credit for pioneering the rap thread on the West Coast. The Sugarhill Gang, Melle Mel, KRS-One, Public Enemy, A Tribe Called Quest, Nas, Dead Prez, X-Clan, and the Wu-Tang Clan all acknowledge The Last Poets for pioneering the art form on the East Coast. Talib Kweli, Common, Mos Def, Grand Puba, Native Tongues, Kanye West, and RBX all regard Gil Scott-Heron with the furtherance of the hip-hop art form through musicianship and poetry.

To date, countless artists have sampled the work of these giants. These elder griots still notice music being released with their unmistakably rapid-fire impression nearly forty-three years after their 1971 releases. The Watts Prophets and The Last Poets have both been an incredible impact on me. Father Amde was one of the first of these giants to take me under his wing and guide me through these tumultuous waters. Father Amde and Jalal Nuriddin have been instrumental catalysts in my later development as an artist.

Expanding the Quilt

As the producer of the spoken-word production *The Still Waters Experience*, which I founded in 2007, I have been afforded the opportunity to get up close and personal with many of the legends from this historic poetry thread. A defining moment for me came when Richard Dedeaux of the Watts Prophets gave the seal of approval for the work we have been producing with *The Still Waters Experience* and The Still Waters Writers' Workshop. Richard also personally passed down a flaming torch of the Watts Prophets' *Talk Up Not Down* workshop handbook so I could carry it forward into our group's journey. With this instructional book, we were able to facilitate our collective from a blueprint of the West Coast's mighty thread.

The Still Waters Writers' Workshop has been in operation since 2010. It has had a steady influx of writers and poets from all disciplines, with the chief aim to grow individually and collectively, while respecting the thread that has parted the sea of poetry, which has given way for our group to assemble. We reverence, honor, and celebrate this momentous thread. In many ways, the yarn of Los Angeles's spoken-word fabric has a direct link to this thread.

The World Stage, one of Los Angeles's premier poetry venues, was the first workshop to dissect my work. Furthermore, every poet that I later taught, facilitated, or guided in any way has become a direct link to this storied thread, knowingly or not, which is in all respects connected to the '65 Watts Writers' Workshop. This thread is my poetry bloodline and the reason *The Still Waters Experience* has consistently shown an appetite to honor poets and artists from this thread in particular.

To date, *The Still Waters Experience* has honored Raspoet Ojenke, Dr. Earl (5X) Grant, the '65 Watts Writers' Workshop, the Watts Prophets, The Last Poets, Amiri

Baraka, Sonia Sanchez, Dee Dee McNeil, Jane Walker, Charles Bibbs, Kamau Daaood, and Riua Akinshegun. We were elated to give them all handcrafted, one-of-a-kind award trophy plaques for their infinite contributions to past, present, and future artists.

We also made it our mission to feature poets that were hosting their own venues at the time. This was to encourage our audience to visit and support other poetry venues in Los Angeles, CA. The list of features and venues included, but were not limited to: Conney Williams (The World Stage), Besskep (A Mic and Dim Lights), Shihan Van Clief (Da Poetry Lounge), Yawo Watts (Oralgasm), Alice The Poet (Spreading Love-N-Spoken Words), Jaha Zainabu (Red Stories), C-Bone Jones (Wordplay), DeanaVerse (Eargasm), Spencer Allen (Poet's Jazz House), and Judah 1 (LionLike MindState). Each of these hosts/poets practiced Umoja (Unity) with me on this spoken-word journey that I have embraced through the years.

The Toast

I would like to now propose a toast—a toast to spoken word! To every ancestor, poet, writer, and spoken-word artist that's in this strand, or has been affected in any way by this strand, I raise my glass to you. To all of the poets and writers that have ever felt the urge to express their ugly, beautiful, and/or indifference with the world, I raise my glass to you. To the women and men that have inspired my journey: my grandmother, grandfather, mother, dad, aunties, uncles, wife, sisters, brothers, elders, homeboys, and friends, I raise my glass to you. To the community of Watts, CA, that has raised me from the Concrete Jungle, taught me, and groomed me for this moment, I raise my glass to you. To all the winos, scholars, drunks, teachers, drug addicts, professors, gang-bangers, and activists from the curbs to the suburbs, I raise my glass to you. This is my poetry thread, a piece of my creative puzzle that I am most honored to have you all be part of.

Last, but not least, I raise two glasses to the reader, the audience, and the supporters of this ancient art form. Thank you for encouraging me, sharing how much my work has changed lives, saved relationships, and helped you on your journey in some small or large way. I will never forget your heartfelt sentiments. I can only hope that this work will inspire you to write, tell your story, and come out the closet with your gifts.

And to all of you secret poets, performing in the mirrors of your bathrooms, those of you who have never been told you can do it, know that you are worthy, validated, and more than enough. You do not need anyone's permission to be great, wonderful, and awesome. Greatness is our birthright! Always remember: I am because you are, and you are because I am. It is so because the Universe says so, and I shall continue to reverence in the energy of this sacred oath, this day, and all the days to come. I accept the charge to share life's beauty, both appalling and apathetic, without reservation, because I am an artist, and we are all artists: Awesome Revealers Transcribers Igniting Splendor Through Synergy. I will never forget who I am; I will never forget who you are; and I will never forget what we are.

Here's to us...   Cheers!!!

Lookin' for Me

If insoever you lookin' for me
Find me 'tween ethers & eons
I'll be portal hop-scotching with Gnostics & Dogons

Spewing an Eastside Swangluish
In Ebonics Medu Neter
Meditating shaman-like
Creating tsunami weather in the cosmos

Do you see me?

Spinning backwards
Inside of an eastern wind
Defending unborn victims of violent crimes
Summonsing family back to tribe
Tribe back to village
Aligning a pilgrimage to self discovery
Blessings are your words
Whenever discussing me!
The Universe hears you...

Find me in Yeshua's DNA
PTAH'S lineage
Practicing black magic for the ages
My legacy ... will be—
Tucked 'tween pages of books too wide to look inside
But keep looking
Open my story
Read me immortal
Remember me as a welder of broken spirits—
That used words to shake   generations
till they wake!

www.poetFood4Thot.com

About the Chef

As a producer, educator, author, and award-winning poet, Oshea (known artistically as Food4Thot) utilizes creative expression to promote the innate greatness that resides in all beings. Coined the "Prince of Poetry" by the late, great Leimert Park poet Dee Black, Oshea's extremely potent delivery is like an iron fist inside of a silk glove.

A native of Watts, CA, Oshea is also the architect behind Lyrical Jinglist, a jingle-writing company he co-founded that writes television and radio jingles for businesses looking to expand into innovative spectrums. He also assembles a quarterly production called Still Waters, featuring dynamic musicians, poets, authors, vocalists, visual artists, African dance, and theatrical skits.

Oshea's passion is working with youth and elders, linking these generations together to better inner-stand the human experience. As a well-regarded facilitator for the Doby Boys youth program in Watts, CA, and the creative-writing coach for EngAGE Seniors Arts Colony in Southern California, Oshea is very hopeful that this link between generations will be repaired through creative expression and unconditional love.

Some of Oshea's work includes (CDs): *Full Course Meal* (2007); *Introducing Lukuma Kwa Luja* (2009); *The Darker Brother Revisited* (2014); and *The Love Lock* (2015). (Theater Plays): *Big City, Bright Lights* (2012). (School Curriculums): *The Still Waters Writers' Workshop* (2010) and *The Super-Heru: Activating Your Super-Hero* (2011). (Books): *Watts Learning Center Anthology* (2011); *Sounds from the Waters Poetry Anthology* (2013); and *Royal Feast: Poetry, Prose & Short Stories* (2015).

With the launch of Still Waters Publishing and Vibrations Holistic Center in 2010, alongside his wife Melanie, Oshea credits his success with having met and learned from many great people along the way.

www.ingramcontent.com/pod-product-compliance
Lightning Source LLC
Chambersburg PA
CBHW032253150426
43195CB00008BA/430